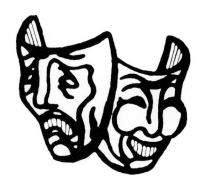

Before My Time

The Story of the
Leicester Drama Society
by John Graham

FOREWORD

It is a few years now since I first agreed to try to write a short history of the L.D.S. The attempt having at last been made, I felt that 'history' would be too grand a word for the product, and I have used a different title.

But I must acknowledge my debts like a proper historian. By far the greatest is to the late Geoffrey Mead, successively Secretary, Chairman and President of the Society, as well as actor, producer and dramatist. From him I received the bulk of the documentary evidence on which I have relied for the early days: Executive Committee minutes, minutes of A.G.Ms., L.D.S. magazines, press cuttings and pictures. Since Geoffrey's time fortunately such records have continued to be kept.

I have made much more use of such printed material than of personal reminiscence, but several members have provided me with anecdotes, for which I am very grateful. I must apologise for not having used all of them: I had to be selective because most people's memories are of theatrical disasters – like the swords that refused to be unsheathed and the guns that failed to go off – and to have included too many of these would have been to suggest that such mishaps have been more common in Drama Society productions than has actually been so.

Apologies too must go to the many members, old and current, who have given valuable service to the Society, both on and off the stage, and remained unmentioned through oversight or misjudgment.

I am grateful to a number of members of long-standing who were kind enough to read my first draft and point out some mistakes I had made; and I must especially thank Lisa Thirlby for her very efficient organisation of the typescript, my wife, Pauline, for Appendix 2 and all sorts of other things, and Paul Whybrow and Edwin Devey for all the technical work prior to printing.

Finally, thanks to the officers and committee for giving me a completely free hand and raising no objection to judgments and expressions of opinion with which they might not agree; and to the Society for being worth writing about and having given me so much pleasure for so many years.

CHAPTER 1

Before The Theatre

On the day after the official formation of the Leicester Drama Society on January 26th 1922 the *Leicester Evening Mail* said this:

"Leicester has, in recent years, seen a remarkable growth of a taste for the drama, expressing itself chiefly in good performances by amateur acting combinations. Those who have the best interests of the drama at heart have for a long time been of opinion that these scattered dramatic efforts ought to be linked up."

This development of an intelligent interest in drama was not peculiar to Leicester, but was one manifestation of a general feeling that the work being done in the commercial theatre of the time – and particularly in the West End – was trivial and mediocre. Many of the characteristics of Victorian drama – improbable plots and cardboard characters, *Boys' Own Paper* moral attitudes, sensationalism and sentimentality – were to be found in the plays of the period; and the flow of musical comedies, inspired by the success of *Chu Chin Chow*, was unremitting.

In contrast to this unhappy state of affairs was the work of the Stage Society and of the Vedrenne-Granville Barker management at the Court Theatre, that of Miss Horniman, who set up repertory theatres in Dublin and Manchester, and of the founders of the Liverpool and Birmingham Reps. In the amateur field we already had Nugent Monck's Maddermarket in Norwich, the People's Theatre in Newcastle-upon-Tyne and Manchester's Unnamed Society. The desire to improve artistic standards in the theatre and to educate public taste was becoming widespread.

With these examples to inspire them, three friends met together in a Leicester café in the November of 1921 to discuss the contribution that Leicester could make to the cause. They were Herbert Pochin, President of the West End Adult School, where much admirable dramatic work was done, Walter Martin, whose Walter Martin Players were well known in the city, and Frank Clewlow, who had recently left the Birmingham Rep., where he worked under Sir Barry Jackson, to seek a less precarious living in the shoe industry. The presence of Clewlow was obviously of very great importance in the foundation and early history of the Drama Society. However experienced and talented in the amateur field the other founder members may have been, it must have added to their assurance to have as a colleague one who was fresh from professional work in one of the foremost theatres in the modern movement.

Since the meeting of these three men was informal, we don't know what was said; but the outcome was a circular sent to leading members of the amateur drama groups already operating in the city asking them to attend a meeting to promote the formation of a society which would combine their strengths. The most important group besides those led by Herbert Pochin and Walter Martin was the Wycliffe Players.

According to the minutes of the inaugural meeting of the Leicester Drama Society it took place in the Permanent Library, though the *Leicester Evening Mail* of the next day says it was held in the Council Room at the Chamber of Commerce. The latter would certainly have been a likely and appropriate venue, for a large proportion of those present were prominent local business men, though there was one clergyman and the Principal of University College, Leicester, Dr. R. F. Rattray, who was elected to the chair. The press report also mentions "influential local ladies".

Dr. Rattray, seconded by Mr. Herbert Pochin, proposed "that a society to be known as The Leicester Drama Society should be formed", and when this proposal had been unanimously carried he outlined the objects which the Society would pursue. According to the account given by the *Leicester Evening Mail* he "pointed out that for some time past it had been felt by many Leicester people that the time was ripe for giving concrete form to a general local growth of interest in better class drama. This desire it was proposed to meet by the formation of a large society which should unite all kinds of support and endeavour".

The formation of a group of producers and actors to present plays was only one of many aims, which included encouraging and advising all kinds of local acting societies, promoting the study of plays as literature and arranging play-readings, recitals, lectures and discussions.

Dr. Rattray may be said to have directed the steps of the infant L.D.S. along the road which it has travelled ever since, when "he laid stress on the condition that on the one hand the society must try to raise the level of dramatic taste in the city, and on the other that it should avoid the excessively 'highbrow'." It would be fair to say that the Society has, over the years, with only slight deviations on one side or the other, upheld solid worth and established merit and looked on the *avant-garde* with suspicion if not distaste.

This middle-of-the-road policy may have been determined by another factor which this first meeting exemplifies. The preliminaries over, the members proceeded to elect no fewer than five sub-committees besides a General Committee. The influence of Frank Clewlow, who was elected as Honorary Secretary at the meeting, was undoubtedly very great in the early days, but the powerful battery of committees and the presence of other forceful personalities must have ensured that he was by no means omnipotent. In the years which have followed the actual number of committees has fluctuated, but the strongly democratic bias has remained.

It has often been argued that an institution like a drama society is best run by an inspired and inspiring dictator, and this may be true of some; but the L.D.S. has never allowed any one man the sole direction of its policies, and the participation of so many in the running of its affairs has led to a sense of shared responsibility which has seen it through some very difficult times.

To illustrate another prophetic note which was sounded, I quote a *Leicester Mercury* columnist:

"A 'Little Theatre' in the Future

"I find that when writing on this topic before I pleaded for

"A building fitted with a proper stage, and with suitable lighting arrangements. This could be let out for a single night, or for weekly or monthly 'runs' . . . The possession of such a theatre by the town would give a great stimulus to amateur acting, to a study of the drama, and to the enjoyment of many onlookers, who would attend to see their friends perform.

"I was pleased to learn the other evening that this is also one of the things the new society has in view – though perhaps in distant view."

Well, not so very distant: it took nine years.

In the meantime plays had to be put on somewhere. The leaders of the Society set their sights high and began negotiations for the hire of the Royal Opera House for a two-week season in the early summer. But the next important event was the Public Meeting, which was arranged to attract a large popular membership and to make the existence and the objectives of the Society more widely known.

This meeting was held on Tuesday, April 11th at the Association Hall. Frank Clewlow had ensured that it would be well attended by persuading Lena Ashwell, the famous actress, to give an address. Though no longer a household name today, she was at the time very well-known and very highly regarded, especially because she had taken a company of actors to France in 1915 to entertain the troops at the Front. She had always been an advocate of high standards in drama and an outspoken, but witty, opponent of the view that the public preferred an inferior article. She condemned those theatre managers for whom the profit motive was the primary concern and spoke warmly of the value of theatre as an emotional educator. She was clearly the ideal person to speak on behalf of a movement the aims of which were so closely in accord with her own, and she must have aroused considerable fervour. Recruitment to the Society was brisk.

A fortnight later the selection of plays for the season at the Opera House was completed. There were to be four productions: Galsworthy's *The Silver Box,* a Triple Bill of one-act plays, *The Fantasticks* by Rostand, and *Candida.* The first three were to be produced by Frank Clewlow and the last by Dr. Rattray. Even when one bears in mind that the one-act plays had been produced before at the West End Adult School and that the principals in *Candida* had played their parts before, it is a remarkable fact that when these final decisions were made the first night of the first play was only seven weeks ahead.

I shall not, later on in this account, be able to mention more than a very small proportion of plays produced, since the number of full scale productions by the L.D.S. is now well over six hundred; but a closer look at this first season will serve to introduce a number of names which are to figure largely in the story of the Society.

The curtain went up on the first play, *The Silver Box,* on Monday, June 12th 1922. In writing of it the *Leicester Mercury* speaks of "a fine presentation of a first-class play", the *Mail* of "an unqualified artistic success" and the *Chronicle* of "a fine well-balanced representation which would stand comparison with the work of professionals". Only the euphoniously named Lentulus Lark, writing in *The Pioneer*, an earnest socialist paper, dissents from the general praise, holding that a playwright as philosophically profound as Galsworthy needs the services of a first-class professional company, and castigates the Leicester audience for its frivolity. Among the players who were to become stalwarts of the L.D.S. in the years which followed were the two leading ladies, Dora Tabberer – who was highly praised by all the critics – and Kitty Holland; William Langley, Frank Toone and Ebb Murray; and in the part of the maid Evelyn M. Hancock, later lovingly known as 'Skinny', who died in 1975 and left a generous legacy to the Theatre.

The season continued successfully from an artistic point of view, though audiences were smaller than might have been hoped and there were few customers in the Upper Circle and the Gallery. In the Triple Bill Frank Clewlow himself appeared in two of the plays, there were three Pochins, Roy, Eric and Elaine, and Albert Northfold. Eric Pochin appeared again, with Harry Letts and H. L. Midgley, in *The Fantasticks*, a play which the *Mercury* critic found too stylised for his taste, with the result that a rather acrimonious exchange of letters peppered the correspondence column of the paper for some days afterwards. Dr. Rattray and his wife played Marchbanks and Candida in the last play of the season, with Walter Martin as Morell and Harry Martin as Burgess. This production seems to have pleased everybody and to have been rather more of a box-office success than the others.

To have organised these four shows in so short a time and to have carried them off with style and confidence was a splendid achievement, which it was generally agreed owed much to the professionalism of Frank Clewlow.

The 1923 season included three plays which ran for a week each. The plays were *The Cassilis Engagement* by St. John Hankin, Galsworthy's *Strife* and *Othello*. Among the names on the programme, in addition to the ones mentioned already, were those of Rita Barsby, Charlotte Buckley, Leslie Bowmar and Geoffrey Mead, who was A.S.M. to R. T. Sault, the chief stage manager to the Society from the beginning and for several years.

The latter was the subject of one of the Society's long-lived anecdotes. Dicky Sault had promised to provide sheets for the bedroom scene in *Othello*, but had left it to the last minute and forgotten. On being reminded of this he rushed out of the theatre and finally returned triumphant. It was later observed that Mrs. Rattray was probably the first Desdemona to die on sheets marked 'Grand Hotel'.

The approach to *Othello* showed that the producer – Frank Clewlow, of course – was well versed in the most modern ideas about Shakespeare production, for it was performed without cuts and with only one interval, the set being so designed, at this period with the help of curtains, that the action could flow on from one scene to the next without interrution. Clewlow played the Moor, and Roy Pochin gave the first of his many performances in major parts for the L.D.S. as Iago.

The next season was the last at the Opera House. It was of two weeks and the plays were *The Merry Wives of Windsor* and *An Enemy of the People*. In March of the following year it was decided on the recommendation of the Business Committee, therefore presumably for economic reasons, that there should be no Opera House season that summer, and from then until the opening of the Little Theatre in 1930 the Society's productions were staged at the unsatisfactory Association Hall (the Y.M.C.A. building on London Road). But in 1924 the L.D.S. had to face another problem – that posed by the resignation of the revered Frank Clewlow, who returned to full-time theatre as producer to the Scottish National Theatre. He had been very much the leader, and his loss was a great shock; but the committee structure was firmly based and there was no lack of talent.

The first producer to fill the gap was Geoffrey Mead, who at the end of 1925 also became secretary. The play he produced was *Outward Bound*, the author of which, Sutton Vane, was engaged to give a lecture to the Society for a fee of five guineas plus railway expenses. The performance was an artistic success and made a profit, but the venue was a bit of a come-down after the Opera House. Geoffrey Mead, writing in a News Calendar of 1955, says of it:

"The productions on this small stage were done under appalling difficulties. All the entrances were from the prompt side only whilst dressing-room accommodation was, according to our present standards, primitive. The flats we now owned had to be taken away after each production and stored in the loft of a private house in the Clarendon Park district."

And a press criticism of one of the productions there has the following passage:

"The limitations of the Association Hall as a theatre are well-known . . . The acoustics play quaint tricks in this hall. In one of the plays, an actor happened to be in the one position on the stage from which the voice 'ricochets' in a peculiar manner, so that for the moment everyone in the circle thought the words were being spoken from the back of it, and many turned round."

So, although the productions of the Society continued to be successful and became more numerous, the acquisition of a theatre of its own became a chief concern of the officers, and the first tentative steps towards this end were taken in 1927. Messrs. Andrew and Ashwell, the estate agents, wrote to say that premises had become available at 51 Northgate Street. The building had previously been a Mission Hall and belonged to the Railway Company, who were prepared to let it to the L.D.S. at an annual rental of £100. It was on a tram route and reasonably central, and seemed to be what the Society was looking for. Then sums were done, and it was realised that a capital expenditure would be necessary, and that the greatest annual income that could be expected (£300) would only slightly exceed the annual expenditure without making any allowance for repairs and renewals.

The scheme was reluctantly dropped, but the determination to acquire a theatre was now firmly established and at the A.G.M. of 1928 the President, now Mr. W. Bastard, "expressed his desire to act in this capacity until he had succeeded in his quest for a theatre for the Society". The Northgate Street Scheme was followed by the Churchgate Scheme, and this by the Crusaders' Hall (Clarendon Park Road) Scheme.

These fell through, as did a plan to buy the Free Gospel Hall in Causeway Lane which seemed to be progressing well until the trustees decided not to sell after all. At a meeting of the Executive Committee in July 1929 a project to build a theatre on another Churchgate site was being discussed when the President was called away. He soon returned to inform the meeting that he had been told that the trustees of the Rechabite Hall in Dover Street would be willing to let the Society have the upper portion of their building on a twenty year lease. This offer was pursued, and six months later to the day the

Little Theatre opened, and a new phase in the history of the L.D.S. had begun.

A great deal had been achieved in those first eight years. Nearly thirty plays had been produced, including a *Hamlet* with Roy Pochin in the lead and a new play, *The Highway*, written by his brother Eric. A programme of three new one-act plays by local authors was the result of a play-writing competition which the society ran in conjunction with the *Evening Mail*. One of the winners was Moyra Haywood. Fairly regular fortnightly meetings had been held and addresses were given by such celebrities as Barry Jackson, William Archer, John Drinkwater, Lord Dunsany and Lascelles Abercrombie. Help had been given to local societies and adjudicators provided for competitions held in the county.

The Drama Society has almost always had quite a good news calendar of some sort, but the Leicester Drama Society Magazine of the twenties and early thirties was a particularly splendid affair. It comprised eight pages every month during the season, properly – indeed beautifully – printed by the Blackfriars Press. It contained very little personal news about members, but a great deal about plays, not only those produced by the L.D.S., but also those which members had seen at the Opera House, in the halls where other amateur groups played, in other Midland theatres and in London. There were articles about dramatists, great actors and actresses and theatrical theory. In short the Magazine represented the Society's expressed intention of furthering the cause of good quality drama. For example, in one issue in 1924 there were articles about Proletarian Drama, Shaw's *St. Joan* and Eleanora Duse, who had just died. In another in the following year there were obituaries of Bakst and William Archer.

Among the most interesting features to us, however, are those which show that all was not always sweetness and light, that the Society suffered sometimes from the rumbling discontents and gnawing grievances which are the stomach upsets of the body theatrical, and that some complaints are chronic. Dr. Rattray, at the end of his presidency in 1925, expressed regret at "the very bad attendance at fortnightly meetings, which he considered a shirking of individual responsibility". There is an article headed "A Grievance" which refers to the Unfair Casting Problem; there is a grumpy editorial which indicates that the Unpaid Subs Problem is perennial too.

I quote from the former:

". . . the question raised [in an anonymous letter from a reader] was one that might interest our readers. The writer complained that few opportunities were given to new acting members, and the inference was that the choice was limited to a select few whenever a play was produced . . .

"It cannot be too strongly emphasised that the sole object of the Society is to present good plays in the best possible way, and we think it may be said that personal considerations do not weigh in the slightest degree. Quite the contrary in fact. The Society still has need of many types of actors."

We can say that – have indeed frequently said it – again.

The same complaint crops up in 1928, in an article in which S. G. Stephenson, a member of the Executive Committee, describes a Members' Night.

"One complaint was voiced, and this was to the effect that there exists among the members many who would like the opportunity to act, but who for some unknown reason, are not approached and never get a chance. From this has arisen the thought that parts are always cast within a select and tried circle to the exclusion of all others . . . Personally I am inclined to think the criticism to be not entirely ill-founded, and I am of the opinion that this may arise from the failure of the Committee to keep an up-to-date register of the abilities and wishes of members in acting matters. Much may be known of the 100 or so who have played in the Society's productions, but there must be many more whose talents are unknown and unused."

In 1929 audition classes were organised and attended by about fifty members.

At the end of the previous season the Secretary had written in his notes:

"During this season we have added a hundred new members, and the number of actors and actresses who wish to be tried out knows no bounds, but in looking back on the shows we have done, not only this year, but last as well, it is obvious that while the casts are constantly changing, and many new faces appearing, the work that is done behind the scenes is carried out by about the same half-dozen stalwarts every time. This is obviously wrong, and as in the season that is ahead of us, a much more ambitious pro-

duction scheme is proposed, it is imperative that members should come forward and volunteer for work in this direction."
Some of that has a familiar ring.

There was a running battle, as there always has been and always will be, between those who thought the Society should do only 'worthwhile' plays and those who thought it was in danger of getting too 'highbrow'. Occasionally a committee member would resign in a huff. But in general enthusiasm and love of the theatre and care for the best possible standards prevailed, qualities which were sharpened by the prospect of the Society's having a home of its own in the new Little Theatre.

CHAPTER 2

The Little Theatre

William Bastard carried out his intention of remaining in office as President until the Society had acquired its own theatre. He had been tireless in his search for suitable premises and his patience and industry were rewarded. As soon as it had been decided to take up the Rechabites' offer, the negotiations with them, together with the organisation of the task of turning the upper part of their building into a theatre, was put in the hands of the President himself, the Executive Committee chairman, Herbert Pochin, and the Honorary Secretary, Geoffrey Mead, assisted by a practical sub-committee comprising themselves, Harry Letts, Eric Pochin, A. H. Davy and William Langley. The outcome of their bargaining with the Rechabites was that the Society was committed to a tenancy of seven years, with the option of two further successive periods of seven years each. A foothold was gained in the lower part of the building and an annual rental of £475 was agreed. Six more sub-committees were set up.

The building which was to be transformed into the Little Theatre had been erected in the nineteenth century and was originally a Baptist Chapel. Like other nonconformist chapels of the period it had had a high, flat ceiling and a gallery round three sides. But in 1919 it was purchased by the Independent Order of Rechabites, who removed the galleries and inserted a raked floor at gallery level. This newly created first floor was to become the auditorium of the new theatre, entered by two staircases which had served the old gallery.

An appeal for funds had already been started in support of one of the earlier schemes which had fallen through, and this was renewed with increased urgency, since it was estimated that the cost of the building's conversion would be £2,500 (as is usual in such matters it turned out to be a good deal more). There were many generous donations, from business men like Percy Gee, for example, from the President, who with Miss E. Frisby defrayed the cost of carpeting the entire floor of the Theatre, and from Russells', the piano people, associated with the work of the Society for many years, who donated a piano. All members of the L.D.S. were, of course, called upon in the strongest terms to make contributions, and most probably did so, though the President complained at the next A.G.M. that there were some who had not.

Further along the road which the Society had taken horrible financial problems lay in ambush, but for the moment the joyous excitement of fulfilling an ambition so long held and striven for must have been the predominant emotion. The Magazine of December 1929, edited for the first time by Mary Waddington following the resignation of the admirable Horace Twilley, bubbled over with happy pride in describing to members the prospect which awaited them.

". . . what shall we see when everything is finished, and we flock to that thrilling first performance of *Hassan*?

"Suppose we are lordly and arrive in Dover Street in a taxi. We step out, at the end of the Rechabites' buildings, where a glass roof projects over the pavement, with lettering announcing that here and in fact is Leicester's Little Theatre. We enter the foyer – box office on our right, and long counter for men's hats and coats on our left. We may expect this to be a really inviting entrance – but how it will be adorned is yet to be decided.

". . . Well then – we are at the top of the stairs and in the theatre. We shall share one thought as we enter – 'Oh, this is *good*'. The theatre gives a sense of being beautifully proportioned – just long enough, just wide enough; and, to be a little more descriptive, having none of that sense of constriction which many of the long, narrow small theatres give . . .

"As a matter of fact, to describe proportions first is not to describe in order the things that we shall see when the theatre is finished. The eye always seizes upon colour first of all. The theatre will be beautifully severe – stone coloured walls, long drab curtains over the windows, soft drab carpet, and rows and rows of full-flame-coloured seats. And then at the end, covering that great wide stage, a brilliant piece of colour, to focus all our attention on the one part of the theatre that really matters – a curtain of shimmering loveliness, in which orange, green, mauve, blue and puce blend dazzlingly . . ."

Eric Pochin's article in the same issue, which describes the working parts of the new theatre, is more sober and more practical:

"The difficult part of a description of a stage is to know where to begin but the thing that is most apparent to everyone is the actual stage opening. In the Little Theatre this is 25ft wide by 15ft high and for the sake of comparison, the Association Hall stage is 22ft wide by about 13ft high . . .

"The curtains are being arranged if possible to draw sideways like those in the modern cinema and also to drop in tableau fashion. It will also be possible to lift them out of sight completely if it is desired for Greek plays or Shakespearean work. From back to front of the new stage or the playing space shows a very decided advantage over previous experience. The limit was about 14ft, now there is matter of about 20ft. This should not only reflect advantageously on the staging but on the players too.

"In the new theatre it will also be possible to 'fly' scenery, which has never been done in the past. This makes scene changing quicker and easier for those on the stage, but also makes a greater range of scenic effects possible for the audience. The height inside the stage is more than twice that of the visible opening, and scenic cloths can be pulled up out of sight, and lowered as required. This is effected by means of a grid of lattice work immediately above the stage on which are fixed pulley blocks and cleats from which the scenery is suspended by ropes. This is, of course, a necessity in any modern theatre.

"Adequate accommodation is provided at the side of the stage for scenery required for a play which is not in use and for 'props' such as furniture, etc., but the main bulk of the scenery will be kept in a room under the stage to which it can be lowered through a trap door in the stage itself . . .

"Among the dressing rooms there is also a room in which the stock 'props' can be stored . . .

"The prompt corner is equipped with the usual signal devices to the orchestra, lights perch, etc., and the electrician is in a position immediately over the prompter so that the two are in constant contact. This brings us to the lighting equipment and as the stage opening is the most obvious thing about a stage so the footlights are the *sine qua non* of stage lighting. In 'the Little Theatre' this will be hardly true, in that these fittings if desired, can be completely hidden by a folding arrangement at the front of the stage. For the producer who does not wish to have the barrier of the 'foots' between his actors and the audience there are three large flood lanterns of a thousand candle-power each arranged for which project from hidden positions in the roof of the auditorium.

"In truth footlights though so obvious are often of least value in stage lighting, so that besides the fitting mentioned above there are three hanging battens of lights. All these are arranged in white, amber and blue, and are fitted with dimmers, so that the volume can be adjusted and raised or lowered at will.

"For local lighting two 'lines' or focus lanterns are situated on perches on either side of the stage but hidden from the audience and for flooding effects of sunlight or moonlight two flood lanterns are just below the 'limes'.

"Odd lights are always required about the stage for lamps or fires, to light ground-rows, doorways or windows and these are provided for, by points or plugs on the floor of the stage, on the 'fly' gallery and so on.

"The lighting scheme has been most carefully considered and it is questionable whether any small theatre in the Midlands will be better equipped considering the cost of the installation under review . . ."

Such then was the theatre, the official opening of which took place on Friday, January 24th 1930.

The platform party included the President, the Lord Mayor, the Chairman of the County Council, and Mr. Geoffrey Whitworth, the secretary of the British Drama League. The speeches, which emphasised the usefulness of the Society in putting on plays which could not be seen in the commercial theatre, were followed by a performance of Oscar Wilde's *A Florentine Tragedy*, which was produced by Geoffrey Mead and acted by Leslie Bowmar, Roy Pochin, Kathleen Haywood and Dorothy Winder. One local paper reporting the occasion describes the theatre as 'a beautiful building with walls and carpet of grey stone, seats of dull orange, gracefully proportioned proscenium arch of an iridescent blue material'. Another says, 'The theatre, which seats 400, impresses with its combination of usefulness and modest luxury'. Mr. Geoffrey Whitworth is reported as saying 'that the stage of the Little Theatre could certainly give points to the stage of eighty per cent of professional theatres in the provinces with regard to the decency and comfort in which the players could work'.

Three days later the first week's run of a full-length play began. The play was *Hassan*, Flecker's beautiful, exotic but rambling poetical drama of the East. It was a daring choice, unlikely to appeal to all tastes, and so difficult in its extravagantly colourful phraseology as to be sure to lead to unevenness in the quality of the performances. Moreover it was knocked off balance by one of those blows of fate which every amateur producer fears. Two or three days before the first night A. H. Davy, who was to play Hassan, was laid low by a sudden and serious illness, and Charles Kinton, instead of playing the Vizier, had to go on in his place carrying a script – at least for the first night. Not surprisingly perhaps the man who stepped in to play the Vizier at very short notice was Roy Pochin. But there were fine performances in the two leading female parts by Doreen O'Driscoll and Dorothy Murmann and as the Caliph by Leslie Bowmar, an excellent actor who played many leading parts at this time and later became theatre manager for a time before finally achieving professional success with the B.B.C. The production was by Harry Letts, who was a representative of a breed which has now become almost extinct: the brilliant but tyrannical producer, not afraid to hurt actors' feelings or send the leading lady home in tears. Both the newspaper criticisms imply that the enforced changes in the cast really did rather spoil the show, but it was a success in that it clearly showed the potential of the Society and of the theatre.

The recollections of two of the actors who took part indicate that the whole operation was a pretty desperate one. This is how Roy Pochin remembered it (News Calendar, November 1957):

"The play was presented under great difficulties. There was very little heating. The stage was like an ice house. We were surrounded by wet brickwork, with only two small radiators to dry it out. And when the curtains opened, the draught blew the hats off the people in the front rows."

The leading man's deputy "had his lines written all over the stage. But the stage was so badly lit he couldn't read them".

In 1972 Leslie Gillot wrote about the production. Leslie has been for many years now the only actor still active who took part in the first production. He recalled some of the same things as Roy, and added this:

"Dress rehearsal is called for 2 p.m. on Sunday and 'no visitors' is the order. We work hard, particularly the back stage staff, as no-one has previous experience on this stage and all is going well until the 'Beggars' i.e. The West End Adult School Gym Class, attempt to exit backwards through a 6ft opening carrying 7ft spears and then CALAMITY. Down comes the huge flat, the auditorium fills with dust, there is a silence and then 'Jafar' speaks his next line, "This is a disastrous situation". However we struggle on but at 2 a.m. Monday although the last scene has not been reached, it is felt that we should stop and we go home."

The seats which accommodated the audience in the new theatre were of two kinds. Most were very decently upholstered, and had cost 22s. 6d. (£1.12½p.) each fixed; but there were four rows at the back of 'a less elaborate and expensive chair', on which the impecunious or thrifty could sit in less comfort. The prices were 3/- (15p) for the best seats, and 1s. 10d. (just over 9p.) for the hard ones and the back row of the comfortable ones. A full house brought in £44 6s. For that first production of *Hassan* the costume bill (for hiring from Simmonds) was £64 17s., which shows the extent to which this was a prestige production which could not be repeated too often.

Four successful productions followed *Hassan* before the end of the season in March, and *The Florentine Tragedy* won first place in the Midlands section of the B.D.L. Area Festival; and if the mood of the A.G.M. in April was subdued rather than triumphant it was for financial reasons. The expenditure on building, furniture and fittings, rates and insurances, etc. had been nearly £4,000. The income from donations to the fund was less than £3,000. There were still bills to be paid and the Society's overdraft at the bank stood at £1,021 6s. 11d. The President urged the necessity for raising £1,600 if possible, or at least £1,200, and a member proposed the appointment of Trustees in whom all the assets of the Society would be vested. This proposal had emanated from the Executive Committee, and there was some difference of opinion with regard to who the trustees should be and how they should be appointed. It is not clear from the records exactly how the matter was resolved, but the appointments were certainly made; and a very worrying time the Trustees had for the next year or two, which seem to have been marked not only by disappointment at the progress of the fund, but by a series of disputes with the Society's landlords. So that in March 1932 we find this paragraph in the Executive Committee minutes:

"... the Chairman reported that as a result of the law suit between the Rechabites and the Drama Society the Trustees of the Society were now virtually owners of the Theatre and Rechabite Hall and offices, they having agreed to purchase the property. Details were not yet decided but Mr. Pochin stressed the necessity of absolute loyalty from the Executive and the Society as a whole to the Trustees in the venture they had undertaken."

The Leicester Drama Society had become not just the tenants, but the actual owners, of their own theatre – so long as they could cope with the mortgage and the overdraft.

The loan which made the purchase of the building possible was from the Rechabites. What exactly, it might be asked, is a Rechabite? And the question is not irrelevant to the future of the L.D.S. The dictionary defines it as "a descendent of Jonadab, son of Rechab, who did not drink wine or dwell in houses" ('But they said, we will drink no wine: for Jonadab, the son of Rechab our father commanded us, saying, Ye shall drink no wine, neither ye, nor your sons for ever' – Jeremiah XXXV, 6). The latter-day followers of Jonadab probably did dwell in houses, but they certainly drank no wine, nor would they lend money to people who sold intoxicating liquors. The Executive

Committee in 1932 had no wish to do any such thing, but the injunction was later to delay the establishment of a bar in the Little Theatre.

CHAPTER 3

Pre-War Years

The early thirties was a time of considerable artistic achievement in the new theatre as well as of financial crisis. A total of eleven plays was produced in the year 1930, and the level of literary merit was, by the standard of the time, which admired Galsworthy, very high. Two of the plays were by him and one by Shaw, there was a successful revival of *Outward Bound*, and two, *The Knight of the Burning Pestle* and *The Shoemaker's Holiday*, were the last plays by Elizabethan or Jacobean playwrights other than Shakespeare to be seen in the theatre up to the time of writing. During the period from late September to Christmas the theatre was operating fortnightly rep. (with one week runs, of course). In the years which followed until 1939 the number of plays never fell below ten and reached the astonishing figure of nineteen in 1935.

The organisation of the Society became much what it is today. An Executive Committee (now called the General Committee) was elected each year at the A.G.M., each member to serve for three years. This then divided itself up into three groups, one sub-committee for Productions (which at that time still included casting), one for Theatre Management (now called Business) and one for Membership Activities. But in 1932, as a result of the Society's economic plight, the legal governing body became the Council.

The Trustees, who made the momentus decision to buy the Theatre, were, besides the President and the Chairman, P. Kendall, Percy Gee, Arnold Viccars, H. H. Peach and Edith Frisby. They deserve mention as much as anyone whose name ever appeared on a theatre programme, for they risked, and I am sure incurred, considerable financial loss as guarantors of the Society's debts before the purchase and, along with S. H. Russell, Percy Russell and H. E. Winks, of the overdraft which had to be sought after the purchase had been made.

The Leicester Drama Society Ltd. was registered as a limited company on 28th September 1932, and the Council, roughly the equivalent of the board of directors in a commercial company, held its first meeting on October 19th. The accountant, Mr. Percy Russell, estimated that the sum required by the Society over and above the necessary mortgage was £9,623, and the contributions and promises already received included £4,830 by the Trustees on opening the scheme. The following two paragraphs from the minutes complete the economic picture:

"The Solicitors were requested to arrange for the completion of the purchase of the Dover St. property from the Independent Order of Rechabites on Wednesday, November 9th, together with the mortgage for £7,500 from the Vendors.

"It was resolved that an effort should be made to collect the whole of the money promised before that date, and to wipe out the existing Accounts guaranteed by individual members, and to substitute fresh Bank Loans for £2,406 0s. 7d., or such other sum as should be required, this loan to be guaranteed by Members of the Council."

There followed a further attempt to raise capital, the issue of a series of 450 4½% Debentures of £10. This should have raised a sum of £4,500 but it never did, for many debentures remained unsold. The composition of the Council was to be five Trustees, as life members, four representatives of the debenture holders and five representatives of the L.D.S. to be elected at the A.G.M. A somewhat reluctant bank manager granted an overdraft of just over £2,000 on the separate guarantees of nine members of the Council.

Frantic efforts were made to raise money. There were repeated appeals to members and to local business men. Five sub-committees worked on the organisation of a spectacular Garden Fête at the De Montfort Hall in June 1933, for which £50 was spent on advertising, two bands were engaged and a firm of caterers was called in. Despite these grand preparations the profit was only about £30, but this result was better than that of the Pageant Play of *Henry the Eight* in the De Montfort Hall Gardens, which was the effort for the next year. This was hit by the weather and made a loss of about £9. Other humbler activities were more successful, but by 1935 the loss of two regular lettings had brought another crisis, which was exacerbated by a sudden falling off in audiences for the shows.

A sub-committee of the Council was forced to recommend that the nine guarantors be asked to pay in the amount of their guarantees and to take debentures in exchange, and stated that an additional £750 would have to be raised as well, saying that ". . . if their suggested proposals cannot be acted upon by the Executive Committee or General Body of Members before 30th June, the only alternative of the Council in the absence of funds will be to vacate the premises . . ."

This was very nearly the end of the L.D.S., at least in the theatre; but at this juncture, or very soon after, an unexpected Fairy Godmother sprang from the wings. This was the Revenue Department, to whom the Treasurer, Percy Russell, had applied for exemption from the Entertainments Tax. They granted this, and even refunded some tax which had previously been paid. This not only saved the guarantors from loss and the theatre from bankruptcy, but cheered everyone up enormously, so that they set about working even harder, if possible, to improve the position. By the end of 1937 a Debt Reduction Fund, culminating in a grand bazaar, called Motley Market, had raised £1,747 9s. 9d. and the Council was able to repay the bank overdraft.

During this difficult period the Society owed much to the guidance of its chairman, Herbert Pochin, one of the three founders, who relinquished the office because of ill-health in 1936 and died in 1945. Geoffrey Mead replaced him in the chair. The presidency also became vacant at this time, and it was taken by Mrs. F. L. Attenborough, the wife of the Principal of University College and mother of famous sons. She was by no means a figure-head and worked most energetically for that vital fund-raising effort.

Meanwhile the shows went on, and the reputation of the Society spread beyond the city. Cecil Chisholm, in a book on *Repertory,* published in 1934, wrote as follows:

"Naturally the amateur repertory director can select much more interesting plays than his professional colleague ... Thus we find the Leicester Theatre Society following *Martine* with Galsworthy's *The Show* as a matter of course in a recent season ... Leicester even takes a Shakespearian play in its stride every year. Incidentally this must be the only amateur repertory which writes, produces and stages an original pantomime at Christmas."

The fact that the set for *Martine* was chosen as one of the illustrations to this book reminds us that the field of stage design (or at least scene painting) is one in which the Society has always striven for, and often achieved, the highest possible standard. Richard Sault, mentioned in connection with the Opera House productions, was still going strong in the thirties and was responsible for both sets and stage management for most of the shows until 1938, when George Kelman took over from him.

The Society in the Little Theatre continued to be very conscious of its duty to present good plays. In an article in the magazine programme (as it had now become for reasons of economy) entitled "Why Amateur Theatres?" the author answers those critics who are scornful of the work of amateurs in the following terms:

"The answer is just as simple as this: Has there ever been a Galsworthy tour in Leicester? Would *Mary Rose* ever have been professionally revived after its first provincial tour soon after its first production? Have the Macdona Players [The company which at that time toured the plays of G.B.S.] ever given *The Devil's Disciple* in Leicester? How many plays of the merit of *The Silver Cord* have been professionally staged in Leicester during this or last season? How much money has been lost on trying to give professional revivals of Elizabethan plays? That is to say, if you want to see plays like the ones the Drama Society has been and will go on giving in Leicester, you have got to make your own arrangements for seeing them – find an amateur cast, find an amateur theatre, amateur stage-hands, and all the rest of the needful people and things.

"If the cast get a little glory out of acting, and having their friends see them in the limelight, they also have to sacrifice a great deal of time, and work very hard, to satisfy the high standard that Drama Society producers expect. And what glory does the stage manager get, or any of his assistants, or the programme sellers, or stewards, or the committee members, or all the other hundreds of people who do a job, often not a particularly exciting job, on behalf of the Society?"

Despite the reference to friends in the audience, there was a growing pride in the fact that the Theatre was now very much a public one, providing entertainment for disinterested people who wanted to see the sort of plays put on there and who found the standard of presentation sufficiently high to justify thier attendance.

In apologising for the winding up of the old monthly magazine and its incorporation in the programme, the editor wrote:

"Members of the Drama Society may perhaps regret a little the change, but they must remember that they now will form only a small part of the audiences at the Little Theatre productions, and that the theatre-going public of Leicester will naturally be eager to know more about the body which has so gallantly undertaken the reponsibility of this lovely little theatre, and which is staging in it plays which would otherwise not be seen in the city.

"Every other week in this theatre the Drama Society is giving a production, which means that practically the full acting, producing, and scene-painting strength of the Society is working nearly continuously throughout the winter . . .

"The old idea must go for ever of 'amateur actors' as people who like dressing up and having their friends to watch them walk the stage, and to hand them up bouquets. An interest in the amateur theatre is a strenuous business these days, and certainly a whole-time leisure occupation."

A programme of 1931 gives an account of how a play was put on at this time which shows some interesting differences from the current practice, and suggests that preliminary planning was perhaps not quite so thorough as producers now try to make it, especially in the field of set design:

"First the play must be cast, and it is no easy task to pick the right one. A special committee functions for that purpose . . ."

Although this has not been the case with the L.D.S. since the war, there are still many Little Theatres which do use casting committees, rather than leave casting entirely in the hands of the producer as we do.

". . . Then rehearsals begin. It is interesting to know that *St. Joan* was only in rehearsal for two months, much broken up by actors being away on holiday. Since we have had our theatre, rehearsals have been far more regimental, and the rehearsal period far shorter owing to the number of plays to be produced.

"After a number of rehearsals in a room, parts begin to take shape, under the direction of the producer, and books are discarded. So to the stage, where actors may 'walk' their parts, get positions right, and begin to feel at home in their parts."

Nowadays the very first rehearsal, except occasionally for a single read-through, is one at which moves are established, though they may, of course, be subject to modification, the theory being that moves and words are inter-dependent and should be learnt together.

"While the actors are busy, the stage manager is beginning to rack his brains about scenery, props, and all the impedimenta necessary to the successful play. The scenery experts confer, and it is decided that certain stock sets may be adapted, and that one or two new ones must be designed specially for the play in hand. A list is made, after reference to the script of the play, of every single property required, and all these must be laboriously found, made or borrowed.

"Lighting plots must be evolved to get the best value from the set, and must be tried out in practice – spots focussed or altered, floods set, foots and battens lit with the right proportion of blues and amber, dimming tried out for effect.

"So at last to the dress rehearsal. Actors must be made up to time, with costumes and wigs coaxed to fit, ready for the producer's eagle eye and full stage lighting."

In the thirties and forties backstage work differed in a number of ways from what it is today. Single-set plays were much less common than they are now, so many more plays required the presence of a fairly large team of fairly large back-stage workers, all capable of quickly and skilfully cleating two flats together. This still has to be done sometimes, of course, but nothing like so often. There were more painted back-cloths and a greater use of black tabs, consequently a greater need for men to work on the fly-rail, which in recent years has only been heavily populated at Christmas time. Nowadays the prevalence of permanent sets, not only for plays where the action is supposed to take place in the same location, but also for classics where slight adjustments are made to indicate change of place, and other plays where two or more locations are on view at the same time and different parts of the stage are isolated by our more sophisticated modern lighting, has led to much more solid construction, and to the bulk of the stage helpers' work being done before the show begins and especially on the Sunday before the final week of rehearsal when the set is put up.

In these earlier days there was no lighting box, but only a lighting perch, high above the stage in the wings on the prompt side – in the Little Theatre, unusually situated at stage right. The lighting personnel had, therefore, a poor view of the stage, and were dependent on very accurate cues from the stage manager. The other major difference in this department was that there was very little front-of-house lighting and footlights were almost always used.

The difference in lighting technique has made, or should have made, a corresponding difference in the application of make-up. The use of the footlights and the overhead batten, one striking upwards and the other downwards on the actor's face, had the effect of making his face a pale, blank sheet. So he started from scratch, giving himself a complexion appropriate to his part, usually compounded of the Leichner greasepaint sticks numbers 5 and 9. Many of us still use these today, though some now use tubes and some pancake, but with modern lighting it is hardly ever necessary to apply make-up so heavily and sometimes it is possible to dispense with a base altogether.

Another, less easily definable, difference between the Theatre before the war and after is a social one. I have hinted when writing about the foundation of the L.D.S. that it was a function of Leicester Society with a capital letter S. A number of people who remember the early years have the impression that most of the leading members – particularly on the acting side – were business or professional people of some means. Indeed, if it had not been so it is highly unlikely that the Theatre could have survived in the form it did. But there is evidence too that the nature of its origins led to a certain exclusiveness which lasted in one form or another for nearly two decades. It was a different world. Dress clothes were worn to the theatre on Friday nights. Leisured ladies were able to devote time to theatre work during the day. Class distinction was much more of a reality, and more than a hint of it was manifest in the Drama Society. I have heard the word "clique" used about the powers-that-were in the early thirties, and the suggestion that there was an established body of leading players who could more or less choose their parts, while newcomers faced a long and uphill battle to gain acceptance. I have mentioned the use of a casting committee, but this seems not to have been consistently applied, and to have given way to autonomy for producers without any obligation to hold auditions; but I will return to the subject of casting later.

A lot has been said about officers of the Society, but a new office must now be mentioned: that of Theatre Manager, someone who would deal with lets and bookings, receive deliveries, find out about rights and royalties, chase up the cleaners, and generally deal with the day to day workings of the Society in the building. In July 1931 Leslie Bowmar was appointed to this position. In 1934, after the Executive Committee had frightened itself by taking on a dauntingly large number of productions in an attempt to make more money, it was decided that a professional producer must be engaged. The man who got the job was J. Rylett Salew from Coventry Rep. Soon after that Leslie Bowmar resigned his post, and the managership was added to the duties of Mr. Salew. Bowmar was retained as a professional player (the only instance I know of such an appointment in the history of the Theatre) and assistant producer. Meanwhile Geoffrey Mead had had to resign as Hon. Secretary in 1932, and Moyra Haywood, who had been his deputy for several years, was elected in his place. Rylett Salew only lasted one year as Manager, and Moyra took on his job as well – at a salary of £100.

She had been a force in the Theatre since the mid-twenties and was wholeheartedly dedicated to it. She was of small stature, with a brisk and lively manner and an amiable – and slightly mannish – appearance. She was a competent, though not an outstanding, actress; and her chief value to the Society was as a producer and as an efficient and tireless organiser. The qualities which distinguished her in her work were her tremendous enthusiasm and the kindness which made her so helpful to beginners and newcomers and so well liked by everybody. If the L.D.S. did not readily open its doors to all who knocked at them, those who were admitted received a warm welcome from Moyra.

To return to the artistic achievement during this decade: I have mentioned the annual Shakespeare productions. These were Birthday celebrations, always performed in April, and all produced by Geoffrey Mead. At that time there seem to have been more actors of real presence, with fine voices, capable of sustaining the big Shakespearian parts, than there have been in recent years. Outstanding among these was Leslie Bowmar; and James Wheeler, himself such an actor, remembers the *Othello* of 1938, in which Bowmar played the Moor, as his favourite among all the Society's pre-war productions. No-one but the finest of critics can ever remember the qualities which distinguish first-rate performance in any detail. The things that stick in the memory are the moustache that comes off on the heroine's upper lip, the doorknob that is left in the actor's hand and the pieces of scenery that fall over; so James's most vivid memory of this excellent production is of Kenneth Harrison's treatment of Lodovico's line in Act V:

"... the one of them imports
The deathio of Cass ..."

Bowmar's Othello was matched by the Iago of Roy Pochin, and the two had appeared with equal success in *Julius Caesar* the year before as, respectively, Cassius and Brutus. Not only fine speaking but also intelligent interpretation always marked the performances of these actors, as this press criticism of *Caesar* suggests:

"Leslie Bowmar makes of Cassius not a conventional villain, but a melancholic paranoiac, and quite rightly. This is a strong and virile performance, which reaches its best in the quarrel scene with Brutus.

"Remains but Brutus. This I always feel, is one of Shakespeare's most difficult parts, so much unsaid must be implied, and Roy Pochin, nobly resisting the temptation to declaim all the time, succeeds in an exceptionally fine study ..."

Arthur Williams was an excellent Mark Antony. Lucius, Brutus' boy servant, was played by an eight-year old actor named Richard Attenborough, who had, the late Geoffrey Mead assured me, a strong Leicester accent. He later appeared as Herald in *Othello* and Second Player in *Hamlet*. This production of *Hamlet* (1939) was, the press reports would suggest, a little less impressive than some of the earlier Shakespeares, but it was marked by one of those rescue acts which from time to time have to be made in the amateur theatre, Rita Barsby having to take over as Gertrude from a sick Kathleen Mead at the last moment and giving a fine performance.

There were a number of outstanding productions by Frank Harwood, a professional producer from The Maddermarket Theatre in Norwich, who had wide experience of work with a number of leading amateur societies, as well as having acted more than once in the West End. He agreed to produce the Pageant Play for a percentage and to direct four other plays for nothing while this was being organised. The first of these was *Journey's End*, and many people who saw this production in 1933 remember it still. It is an extremely moving play (which still works in the theatre, as a recent revival showed), and it was brilliantly performed, with Gordon Salmon as Stanhope. Another was Somerset Maugham's *Sheppey*, an example of a fine acting performance by Geoffrey Mead, who figured more often as producer, and the occasion of a substantial letter from the author to Harwood, who had asked him for an explanation of the appearance of Death to the hero in the guise of a prostitute. Frank Harwood also added to the sum of the Society's classical revivals with fine productions of *The School for Scandal* (1937) and *The Way of the World* (1936).

Lady Precious Stream (An old Chinese Play done into English according to Traditional Style) was a very interesting novelty in 1935. This charmingly mannered play, with actors coming forward to explain their roles to the audience, came fresh as a sea breeze in a theatre which had its own conventions, like the acceptance of painted bookcases, but saw very little stylised work. It must have been one of very few – if any – productions not played in a box set. The producer, Doreen O'Driscoll, a very prominent member during the thirties, also played the lead, a practice frowned upon nowadays.

Geoffrey Mead revealed yet another accomplishment when his own play, *Nine Days Wonder* – a dramatisation of the tragic story of Lady Jane Grey – was produced in 1934. The critics had some reservations about the performance, but the writing was highly praised; and it is interesting to read the comments of the society columnist of the *Evening Mail* on the first night as a social occasion:

"It was like a London first night. Practically the whole audience was in evening dress, which, of course, added to the success of the evening.

"The Lord Mayor and Lady Mayoress of Leicester, Alderman and Mrs. E. Grimsley, were present, and others in the civic party were the Deputy Lord Mayor, Alderman W. K. Billings, who was accompanied by her daughter, Mrs. Byford, who wore a grey squirrel coat over her evening gown . . .

"I have never seen so many leading ladies of the Drama Society actually watching the performance . . .

"Among the amateur actresses were Miss Fanny Lorimer, looking very charming in cinnamon brown and oyster, Miss Marion Pickard, in blue ring velvet, who was accompanied by Mr. and Mrs. J. G. Pickard and Miss Doreen O'Driscoll, a dainty figure in pale green striped satin and a white fur capelet, Miss Marjorie Elkins, who had a fur coat over her evening gown, Miss Helen Bassett looking striking in a black and green ensemble, and Miss Kitty Holland in black and beige lace.

"There were many more, but in the packed audience it was difficult to pick them out. Miss Moyra Haywood, the popular secretary, was as busy as ever."

In the next season Geoffrey Mead followed up his first play with another historical reconstruction, *Charles Rex*, which seems to have been a success in every way, with a fine performance by Leslie Bowmar in the lead. Then he tried his hand at satirical comedy with *Remember Sparta* (1938), set in an imaginary modern country. A much broader sort of satire had been attempted in the previous year by another member-author, Eric Pochin, who had written several pantomines and now offered "a flippant and entirely unreliable History of Leicester" called *Semper Eadem*, which seems to have been very funny.

Many other brilliant successes could be mentioned, and undoubtedly the decade which followed the opening of the Theatre was one of remarkable achievement, particularly when one views in retrospect the awesome series of threats to its existence which the Society had to counter. That there were shortcomings is equally certain, and it is interesting to consider what form these usually took. An article entitled "Annual Stocktaking", which appeared in the Magazine in

January 1939, unsigned, and therefore the work of the editor or the Secretary, contained the following assessment:

"About the plays which we have performed during the first half of the season there have been the usual grumbles. Looking back over them certain comments seem obvious. *In Theatre Street* was an unfortunate choice for the commencement of a new season. People could not make head or tail or if and their bewilderment was not lessened by the comic-opera conception of the Board-room of a Film Corporation. I still feel this conception must have possessed some peculiar subtlety that I am too doltish to perceive. *Boyd's Shop* neither deserved the acid criticism it received nor the defensive protest inspired by that criticism. It didn't matter very much either way. *Remember Sparta* bore the stamp of careful production and the interest of being an original play by a member of the Society. *The Road to Rome* received the competent acting, beautiful costumes and good lighting that such an excellent play deserves. *Dangerous Corner* unfortunately did not.

"But a word about the acting. The honours without a doubt go to Kenneth Mackintosh for his performance as Hannibal, but so many other *new* acting members have appeared this season that further distinction is invidious. And there is a great deal of very useful promise among this new acting talent. A rather heavy share of the responsibility for production has fallen on Miss Haywood, who was connected with four out of the five shows before Christmas. It is a great pity that the Little Theatre cannot offer a 'training ground' to both producers and actors . . ."

This does not suggest an atmosphere of uncritical complacency; but a hostile critic – though himself an active member – writing only a couple of months later, can still say:

"I have, in the past, been accused of insincerity, uncharitableness, and wilful malice towards the Little Theatre, because in one or two programme articles I have departed from the conventional habit of flattering that self-satisfaction which is a steadily growing cancer in the very heart of our Society."

The writer of this was Falconer Scott, a volatile, creative young man who joined the Society in the late thirties. He used his energy to some purpose, setting up a Playgoers' Club to encourage new talent – they performed one of his own plays – and prodding the authorities unmercifully to get them to cast their net wider for players and producers. Bearing in mind then that he was adopting a warlike posture and possibly exaggerating a little with a view to shaking up the Society for its own good, I should like to quote the rest of his article at some length, because it does seem to point out some real weaknesses. Having criticised the choice of plays on the grounds that, while rejecting 'thrillers' as too lowbrow and experimental plays as too highbrow, there was a tendency to settle for an undistinguished type of light comedy, he goes on:

"Many fine plays are turned down, 'because we haven't anyone to play the lead'. Who knows? The system of casting is so patently absurd that it is almost by accident that new talent is discovered. If, instead of grabbing as much as possible of the known experience available, and casting plays 'to type', our producers held play-readings, encouragement and experience would be given to young members, and greater versatility be found in established actors whose full abilities at present remain untapped. But this is not the only evil. By playing for safety with 'type casts', and compelling most of the 'stars' who can spare the time to play leapfrog through the season, the rehearsal time possible for each production is limited to ten or eleven days. This means that detail is sacrificed, and producers cannot afford to spend time training inexperienced actors who consequently do not improve as they should from one performance to another. Even with an experienced cast a play does not really take shape (that is the actors are not comfortable in their parts) until half-way through the week..."

There seems to be contradiction between the first writer's claim that many new actors had appeared during the season in question and what Scott has to say about the casting. The explanation probably is that while there was a tendency at this time for leading parts to be offered automatically to established members of the Society, a number of plays with large casts were performed during this season, so that there was plenty of opportunity for newer members to appear in smaller parts. Certainly there does not seem to have been any regular system of holding auditions for individual plays or of inviting applications for parts.

Falconer Scott goes onto say, "It is also a distressing fact that eleven of the fourteen plays this season have been shared by only two producers, and, although I am not prepared to say that they would have been better produced, I do feel it is a mistake not to renew the reserve of producers which has been greatly depleted during the last few years."

But this was 1938/9, and the war was soon to change everything.

The reference to the shortness of rehearsal periods is staggering. It can hardly be true that all productions were put on in so short a time; not, for instance, the annual Shakespeare, nor a number of other productions which evidently reached such a remarkably high standard that they must have been very thoroughly prepared; but that any play could be staged after rehearsing for less than a fortnight is almost unbelievable to us today. After the war four weeks was regarded as an absolute minimum, and for many years now the usual period has been either five or six weeks, and longer than this for large-scale productions like a Shakespeare or a pantomime.

In that last season of the thirties business was bad for the Little Theatre as it was for the entertainment world generally. The international situation did not seem compatible with any kind of frivolity. But theatre people keep trying, and in an attempt to make up for the financial loss which had been incurred the L.D.S. staged a special end-of-season production of *The Doctor's Dilemma* which ran for four nights and included in the cast Anthony Harris, a leading man who returned to give a number of distinguished performances after the war, Walter Martin, Kenneth Mackintosh, Marian Pickard, James Wheeler and Jack Ayling. Moyra broadcast a talk about the Society's work on Midland Regional from Birmingham, and there was also a broadcast of *Boyd's Shop*. Geoffrey Mead had his play, *Remember Sparta*, performed by Coventry Repertory Theatre. The Annual Dinner-Dance was held in April at the Bell Hotel (tickets 8/6, Dance only 5/-).

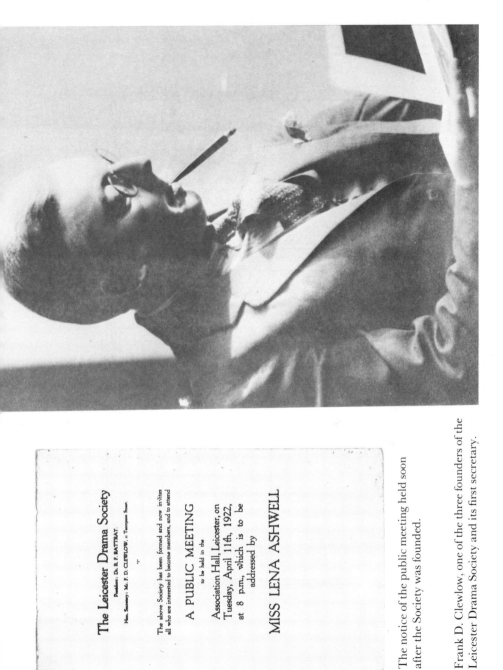

The notice of the public meeting held soon after the Society was founded.

Frank D. Clewlow, one of the three founders of the Leicester Drama Society and its first secretary.

The LEICESTER DRAMA SOCIETY MAGAZINE

VOL. 1. No. 6.   FEBRUARY, 1924

FORTHCOMING MEETINGS

MONDAY, FEBRUARY 18th

MR. WILLIAM ARCHER will speak on "CONSTRUCTION AND TECHNIQUE IN PLAY-WRITING"

MONDAY, MARCH 3rd

A READING OF "SHAKESPEARE" A PLAY IN FIVE EPISODES BY H. F. RUBINSTEIN AND CLIFFORD BAX

MONDAY, MARCH 17th

PROFESSOR LASCELLES ABERCROMBIE will speak on "THE CASE FOR POETIC DRAMA"

All the above MEETINGS in The Edward Wood Hall at 8 p.m.

ORCHESTRA.—*The next rehearsal will be at 7 p.m., on Thursday, February 21st, at The Church House, 5 St. Martin's East.*

SUBSCRIPTIONS *are now very much overdue. Will all members who have not yet paid, kindly make a point of doing so at once?*

INDEX

Front cover of one of the magazines produced regularly throughout the 'twenties.

Covers of two of the programmes for plays produced at the Association Hall.

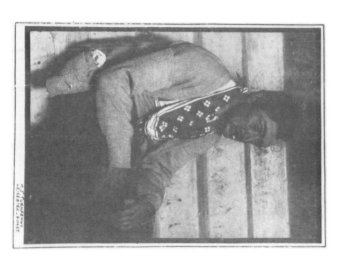

Geoffrey Mead as Alonzo in
A Hundred Years Old (1930).

The Leicester Drama Society presents

"HAMLET"
By WILLIAM SHAKESPEARE

The most ambitious local production of recent years

Roy Pochin as Hamlet (handbill), 1927.

CHAPTER 4

The War and the Peace

The 1939 Autumn season did not get under way. In those early days of the war harmless unnecessary things automatically shut down, as rabbits disappear into their burrows at the whiff of a predator. After a few months heads began to re-emerge.

Fourteen plays had been chosen for 1939/40, but in September Geoffrey Mead, as Chairman, told the press that the theatre and premises of the L.D.S. would be entirely closed down, so as to save expense of rates and maintenance; but that the management would explore any scheme that might show a way to produce revenue.

The theatre remained closed for six months, by which time something had turned up, and the Little was able to open its doors again with only another of its cat's lives lost. What had happened was that the Y.M.C.A. had taken over the lower halls and was paying a rent of £150 as well as bearing a proportion of the standing expenses. Moreover, the Y.M.C.A. hall had closed down, which improved the prospects of letting the Theatre to other organisations. Moyra Haywood was recalled at a salary of £150, and it was agreed that activities should be resumed on a trial basis with one play a month. So in April 1940 *Jane Eyre* was staged, with Jean Ironside as the heroine and Gilbert Gillard as Mr. Rochester. On the first night of this first war-time production the house was full and about a hundred people had to be turned away. Four more plays were given during the year, and the Society presented a production by the Leicester Operatic Players of *The Gondoliers*; but the latest worry was, of course, the gradual draining away of man-power as one member after another joined the forces. For this too fortune provided at least a partial remedy in the establishment in Leicester of a sizeable unit of the R.A.P.C. I quote from the programme for *Laburnum Grove* in November 1940:

"The Royal Army Pay Corps, which has formed a very active and enthusiastic Dramatic Society among its members, has already put on one show and plans are in hand for at least two future productions. The Drama Society feels itself indebted to their acting members also in rather a special way. They have come along willingly to swell our ranks depleted by the war. It is a fine spirit and we acknowledge these services most gratefully and thank them for helping us to people our stage."

Throughout the war the Pay Corps continued to make a substantial contribution to the Society's income by hiring the theatre and to supply all-important male actors. Names which are still remembered from among them are those of Arthur Castledine, who was a fine bass singer as well as an actor, Lister Beck, a good-looking leading man, and Roy Moir, an accomplished comedian and farceur.

Another soldier to appear at the Little Theatre was Lt. 'Jimmy' Clifton James; and it was here that he first did the impersonation of Field Marshal Montgomery, whom he closely resembled, which led to his being sent to various theatres of war to mislead the Germans as to Monty's whereabouts.

In the Autumn of 1940 came a direct threat to the existence of the Theatre in the form of an enemy air raid. An incendiary bomb dropped on the building, but this was promptly and gallantly extinguished by Moyra Haywood, who climbed into the roof with a stirrup pump. Windows were broken, doors were blown in, and a patch of scorched ceiling was left, which remained until it was painted out five years later. Incidents of this sort – though not common in Leicester – discouraged attendance at the theatre; the enthusiasm evident at the opening dwindled, and programmes continued to plead for greater support:

"We know theatre going is not easy these days but it is often more invigorating than an hour or so spent by the fireside expecting the worst to happen when nothing happens at all!"

From 1940 until the beginning of 1943 the conduct of the Theatre was entirely in the hands of Moyra Haywood, in conjunction with Percy Russell as Treasurer and representative of the Council. With one early exception she produced all the sixteen plays that were staged during this period. These included two of the Priestley 'time' plays, which were enjoying a considerable vogue, revivals of plays by Galsworthy and Drinkwater, and Robert Ardrey's *Thunder Rock*, an intelligent, stimulating play set in a lighthouse, which tried to examine, through an interesting, if contrived variety of characters, the problems which faced the intellectual confronted by the prospect of a world war. There were two Christmas productions of *What Happened to George*, the second of which, in 1943, was followed by an extra holiday show, *Treasure Island*.

In the latter Jim Hawkins was played by John Attenborough, youngest of the three brothers, and the now more famous David appeared as a pirate. Hanns Freutel, later known as Paul Hansard, doubled as Black Dog and Ben Gunn. Trevor Thomas, the curator of the Museum, played Dr. Livesey, and Harry Martin was Long John Silver. He also co-produced, assisting Moyra Haywood, and this was the last production that bore Moyra's name.

Despite the onset of illness, she had carried on working on her last two shows, but by February she was too ill to continue. All her work was deputed to her friend and helper for many years, Marian Pickard; and Fred Julian was asked to act as Deputy Theatre Manager, taking charge of most of the administrative work. Soon afterwards Moyra died, plunging the society into mourning.

Everyone was determined that what she had done for the Theatre should not be forgotten: her enthusiasm in the early days, her leadership in the thirties, and especially her work in keeping things going during those last three difficult years. A fund was set up to raise a memorial to her, in the form of a downstairs clubroom which still bears her name today. More than £700 was collected. In September 1943 a Memorial Masque, entitled "Curtain Call" incorporating scenes from L.D.S. successes, with linking material written by Trevor Thomas, was performed by as many leading members of the Society as were now available.

Geoffrey Mead wrote an obituary for the next theatre programme, which contained these words:

"What with theatre management, play production and acting, not to mention lecturing engagements elsewhere, Moyra's life was a strenuous and busy one, but she was never too busy to give helpful advice to all who approached her, however trivial the request or however tiresome the interruption.

"This Theatre will miss her smile, her thoughtfulness, her foresight, her energy and above all her complete unselfishness, more than any of us dare to acknowledge, but the thought of her must prove a spur to our endeavours and a challenge to us, and incidentally to you who read these words, to keep the curtain up in good times and bad."

Marian Pickard, an actress of authority, had co-produced four plays with Moyra before the war, the first of which was *The Old Ladies* in 1937, and for some time she had been her assistant also in the management of the Theatre. She was tall and elegant, a typical English Lady in dress, speech and manner, but subject to spasms of artistic temperament – a somewhat formidable character at first meeting. But like Moyra, she was capable and well-liked and carried on efficiently after Moyra's death.

By now things were beginning to return to pre-war proportions. The annual meetings were resumed. A full General Committee was elected, with Flying Officer Geoffrey Mead as its chairman. For the first time since 1939 an appeal for new members was made – in the programme for *Dear Octopus* (August '43), Marian Pickard's second solo production. The subscription was now set at 7s. 6d. (37½p.), and everyone was invited to a party in the autumn. Frank Cooper Watson was appointed Membership Secretary, an office he was to hold for many years.

In April 1944 the Society decided to employ a professional Director of Plays and co-manager, and the job was given to John Bourne. He was a man of the theatre of some reputation, a well-known adjudicator of drama festivals, an editor of plays and one-time dramatic critic of *The Times*, *The Observer* and *The Liverpool Post*. But he produced only two plays for the L.D.S., *A Midsummer Night's Dream* and *The Rose and the Ring*. One thing he did do, as soon as he took up his appointment, was to try to bring fresh talent into the theatre. He invited anyone who wished to attend an audition 'prepared to give two pieces of their own choosing, preferably in contrast'. This bore some fruit. He advertised an Acting Course for the summer, called "The Theatre in Theory and Practice", and he tried to set up a Shakespeare Club; and lastly he invited the submission of new plays in competition, promising production and royalties for the one adjudged the best.

But his experience with the Little Theatre was not on the whole a happy one. I have written already that the L.D.S. never came under the sole leadership of one person. Moyra's work at the beginning of the war, though lonely, was really the carrying out and extension of policies laid down in co-operation with others. John Bourne, on the other hand, came to the Society from outside and was given a title which suggested that he would be able to wield autocratic power;

and, as an acknowledged expert in his field, this is what he would have expected to do. I surmise that he found it otherwise, that his judgements may have been questioned and his decisions subject to ratification by committees. To the Society he may have seemed less competent in the practical running of a theatre than able as a theorist. This is what he wrote in the magazine "Amateur Theatre" six years later:

"As for the Little Theatre, may God save me from most of them with their pretentiousness and immaturity. Yet the idea is right – that of a home in which amateurs can work, experiment and gain knowledge. I have enjoyed The Questors, Great Hucklow and Leicester Little Theatre in spite of the many unhappy times at the last-named, due I think to a clash between three forces (to be found in most of these 'little' ventures) namely the old, the ultra-new and the common-sense."

A clash of personalities there certainly was; and in 1945 Bourne intimated to the Council that he did not wish to continue for a second year, though he was prepared to act as a consultant. In the previous November Marian Pickard had had to resign owing to ill-health.

Fred Julian, who had not up to now been paid for his services, offered to act as full-time manager. The Council agreed to this when they found that Roy Pochin was able and willing to accept the office of Honorary Secretary. Fred was to deal exclusively with the business side of the Society's affairs and to receive a salary of £300.

This was to prove a long-lasting arrangement. Fred was one of the great characters of the Theatre, and until retirement in 1961 he served the Society with complete dedication, working absurdly long hours. He was a small, wiry, bald-headed Lancastrian; a man of enormous energy, with a touch of acerbity in his manner which sometimes offended those who did not know him well, but a generous and helpful nature beneath it which made him hundreds of friends among those who did.

Poor Fred was always having his leg pulled because of his grumbling about lights not being switched off, particularly the individual make-up lights beside the mirrors in the dressing room. And I find a minute of a Council meeting in the year of his appointment which deplored the high cost of electricity and called on the General Committee to economise in every way possible. Obviously this must have made a deep impression on Fred and he never forgot it.

With the appointment of a manager who was a business administrator rather than an artistic director the responsibility for the choice, direction and production of plays now reverted to the General Committee, with whom it has remained, though the committee has not since the thirities been responsible for casting, which is left to the individual producer.

Much better rehearsal facilities became available again when the Y.M.C.A. vacated the lower rooms in 1947, and two things happened to improve the economic position of the Society: it was recognised as a charity, and therefore exempt from income tax, an annual saving of some £400; and the interest on the mortgage was reduced from 5% to 4%.

With the death of Moyra and the departure of Marian Pickard there was a need for more producers. This need was filled for two or three years mainly by the Martin brothers, Harry and Walter, by Emmie Bent and A. E. Christopherson.

Walter had not produced for the L.D.S. since the mid-thirties, and Harry, though an active member of long standing, had never done a production before he stepped in to help Moyra with her last play, *Treasure Island*. He was a good producer, who got results, but he did have a reputation for losing his temper. However, he was not ruthless like Harry Letts; and it was generally agreed that he could not help his rages and he was forgiven. The sparks flew most colourfully when his brother Walter, who always had his own ideas, was playing for him.

Emmie Bent had been on the fringes of the L.D.S. since the early days, occasionally playing small parts and doing a lot of work with the Vaughan Players. Roy Pochin recognised her great ability, as others had not, and drew her more completely into the Society. She was a more-than-competent producer, who did well with both Shaw and Chekhov, but it was as an actress that she is best remembered. She played many leading parts – and others most willingly if required – with great sincerity and warmth. Her interpretations were always thoughtful and subtle, with carefully balanced light and shade.

In 1945 the sad news was received of the death on active service of Major Maurice Westhead, a talented and witty man who had been the County Librarian. He was an actor of distinction, who gave a particularly fine performance as Napoleon in *St. Helena* by R. C. Sherriff and Jeanne de Casalis; and he was responsible for three productions, including the last in the official 1939 programme, de la Roche's *Whiteoaks*. Another L.D.S. player who was killed in action was Clifford Ryland George, a prominent member for some years before he joined the forces.

As the war drew to a close and V.J. Day followed V.E. Day the men began to come back from the forces. In 1945 the number of plays produced rose to eleven again, some of them with large casts, like *In Good King Charles's Golden Days*, and the play which had been chosen as the best from among the new plays sent in, Leslie Walker's *Drum on the Shore*. Everyone was delighted that the winning play should have been written by one of our own members. It dealt with the relationship between Elizabeth I and Francis Drake, before the time of the Armada, with Pauline Smart as the Queen and Leslie Bowmar as the seaman.

An outstanding performance of 1946 was that of Marie Villiers in Housman's *Victoria Regina*, a severe test for an actress, in that it spans the whole of the Queen's sixty glorious years. Another (in 1947) was in *The Light of Heart*, produced by Geoffrey Mead, who had finished the war as a squadron leader. The lame heroine, in a play which can come across as maudlin unless exactly the right note is struck, was beautifully and movingly played by Margaret Ashwell.

The Society also staged another of Geoffrey Mead's plays, this time one based on his own experience in the R.A.F., *Dust Among the Stars*. It bore some resemblance to *Outward Bound*, since the central group of characters, the crew of a bomber, turned out to be dead. The Captain was played by John Sumpter, who was a juvenile lead in great demand at this time and then left the Society for some years to return – a leading man now – in 1965.

Three years later came the last of Mead's plays to be produced by the Society, *Portrait of a Queen*. This was another Elizabeth play (Dorothy Winder this time), which had been written some years previously, and, after prolonged negotiations, only just missed being put on in London.

In 1946 we were asked if we were interested in joining in the formation of a guild of Little Theatres. A draft of the aims and objects was received, and in June the Secretary proposed that we become founder members of the newly formed Little Theatre Guild of Great Britain at a yearly subscription of five guineas and that we send a delegate to the forthcoming conference in Bradford. A month later Fred Julian presented a report on it, listing the ways in which it was hoped member theatres would be able to help one another – with royalty problems, scripts, exchange of information on methods of rehearsal and business management, etc. Membership of the Guild was to be confined to societies which controlled their own theatres, and the other founder members were Bradford Civic, the Crescent (Birmingham), Great Hucklow Village Players, Highbury L.T. (Sutton Coldfield), The Maddermarket, The People's (Newcastle-upon-Tyne), The Questors, the Unnamed Society (Manchester), The Compton Stage Society (Shaw), The Loft (Leamington Spa), the Stockport Garrick and Newport Playgoers (Mons.). There are now about forty members. As Membership Secretary Frank Cooper Watson began attending the conferences (three a year) regularly, and he continued to do so, missing only one or two, for the next thirty years.

An interesting sidelight on productions in the immediate post-war period is that for many of them – ordinary plays – we still employed live musicians. For instance, it was agreed (a committee minute) that the Blockley Trio should be engaged for *St. Joan* (1946), which they preluded with a performance of the *Capriol Suite* of Peter Warlock, following this during the intervals with works by Rameau and Couperin. Constance Blockley and her colleagues played in fact for almost all productions during this season, but the inexorable march of progress was signalled by the acknowledgement in the *Victoria Regina* programme: "Music selected and arranged by Douglas Goodlad and David Compton and recorded by the 'Unique Sound Reproduction Co.'".

The 1947/48 season was a notably successful one. A voucher scheme had been introduced, selling a set of tickets to patrons at a reduced rate, and this had increased attendance at the plays. The membership now stood at 621 and the profit on the season was nearly £600. Thirteen plays had been produced, each by a different producer, a very different state of affairs from that prevailing before the war.

CHAPTER 5

Consolidation

From this point – the autumn of 1948 – the nature of this story changes, since it ceases to be 'before *my* time'. Up to now what I have written has been based on documents and other people's recollections. From now on the complication of my personal involvement could lead to a degree of distortion. In making value judgements about the quality of productions and performances I shall wish to avoid giving offence to friends and colleagues on the one hand, and being too gushingly adulatory on the other.

Since 1948 the Society has staged some four hundred full-scale productions, so it will naturally only be possible to mention individually a very small proportion of these. I shall therefore restrict myself, as a general rule, to successful productions, taking as the criterion of success the number of times a play was mentioned in a questionnaire sent out to members asking them to say which had impressed them most.

I hope, though, that the lack of reference to failures will not be taken to mean that I think there have been none. Over the years we have, of course, like any other comparable organisation, had our quota of inept productions and inadequate performances. I can most safely illustrate this from my own experience. I have been responsible for fifteen full productions, with ten of which, though they could have been improved in certain particulars, I have been reasonably well satisfied. With the other five I have not. The reason for dissatisfaction, apart from my own shortcomings, has usually been that I have made a mistake in casting, or that I have not been able to get hold of a suitable person to play an important part. Obviously this happens quite often to others as well. When a play is chosen by Productions Committee there may appear to be two or three members who would be capable of playing a certain difficult leading part. When the producer comes to cast the play he may well find that none of these people happens to be available, for this is an amateur society and nobody is under contract; so he must approach a fourth and then perhaps a fifth choice. Sometimes the fifth choice surpasses all expectations and gives a brilliant performance; sometimes not.

There are other causes of failure too: the producer's own errors of interpretation or lack of imagination; an unfortunate choice of play; even a bad stage manager; with the natural result that there are shows which we prefer to forget. I hope I shall be forgiven if I do not tell you which I think they were. Other plays, however, stay in the memory for reasons which have nothing to do with their merit or lack of it.

The production above all others with which old hands who were in it have bored new members, and anyone else who could be persuaded to listen, was *Richard III* (1949). It was neither a particularly good nor a particularly bad one, but it was undeniably – though exactly why it is hard to say – memorable.

The producer was Frank Harwood, the visiting expert who had done so much for the Theatre in the thirties. I think we all liked Frank and admired his work, but we found him distinctly odd, partly perhaps because he addressed females as 'darling' and males as 'dear boy', a practice common enough in the professional theatre, but unheard of in the L.D.S., at least since the war. Also he had a splendid line in fanfares, delivered through cupped hands, which a mistimed entrance could reduce to bathos. He was not at all bad tempered, but the incompetent attempts of raw recruits to the stage to die in the right place or run down some steps without actually falling over would sometimes bring him to a state of despairing frustration which had a humorous aspect to an objective observer.

Richard was played by David Lyall, a protean actor of great versatility, at his best in comedy. He was very good, and didn't play the hunchback king for more laughs than is legitimate; but he always saw the funny side of things and kept everyone amused. Most of us had more parts in *Richard* than we normally got in a year, and the passage to and from the dressing rooms to enchange bits of crêpe hair and costumes often verged on the frantic.

The most amusing single feature of the production arose from an unaccountable aberration in design. For the battlefield scene each of the opposite downstage wings was occupied by half a tent. These half-tents were not particularly large, just big enough apparently to house a G.O.C. and his adjutant; but from time to time a sizeable army would emerge from them, flourishing broadswords and pennants, as from a Dr. Who police-box.

This scene, and especially the bit where the assembled soldiery knelt to the victorious Richmond, presented great difficulties at the later rehearsals; and we spent so long with one knee pressed down on the reticulations of knotted string which passed for chain mail that we bore the indentations for days. Perhaps it was such discomforts as this that gave to playing in *Richard* a gentlemen-in-England-now-abed feeling.

One member of the cast of *Richard III* who might, speaking with hindsight, have been expected to add to the general risibility was Joe Orton, then known as John Orton, who played a messenger; but the young man whose contribution to theatrical life was later to be so hilarious, outrageous and dramatic was at this time sixteen and still feeling his way in the world, and is not remembered as having done anything to amuse or shock – is not in fact very clearly remembered at all.

The idea was now established that the Society had, and would use, many different producers, and this has been maintained; but there have, of course, always been one or two who were regarded, tacitly at least, as the best of the current bunch. Nevertheless it has been rare even for them to take on more than two shows in a season.

The post-war producer to emerge as successor to Geoffrey Mead, the Martins and the Pochins was Geoffrey Burton, who made his debut in 1948 with *The Shining Hour*. He was a very sensitive director of players, very aware of the nuances of meaning and feeling in the author's text, meticulous over detail, worrying away at a passage which did not seem quite as it should be until he got it right.

Himself an able writer of sketches and light lyrics, he produced in 1949 one of the best revues to be staged by the Society, *Little by Little*; one of the best because the music, by Frank Smith and Roy Wright, as well as the script, mostly by Burton, was original. Some of the numbers are still remembered – in particular the one about the three statuettes, The Whistling Boy and The Cherry Boy and The Little Girl So Shy, and The Three Victorias (Falls, Park and Station). Geoffrey was well served by such fine comedy players as David Lyall, Pat Marcham, Marie Villiers and June Mansell.

In the following year Geoffrey Burton produced a play which has proved equally memorable, Thornton Wilder's *Our Town*. Perhaps it was partly the quality of the play itself which made it linger in the mind while other admirable productions were forgotten; but certainly the staging was beautifully stylised, and one remembers particularly the scene with the boy and girl on top of the stepladders which represented their opposite bedroom windows. The girl was Ruth Elliott (later Berridge), making a delightful first appearance – happily to be followed by many more – for the Society; the boy, Peter Hollins.

One of Geoffrey's more bizarre productions was the 1950 Christmas pantomime, *Sinbad the Sailor,* the first half of which was written by himself under the influences of ITMA and Much Binding in the Marsh, and the second by Eric Pochin in the manner of H. J. Byron. It was quite fun despite this schizophrenia, but it did not start a fashion for panto. It took another fifteen years, and another producer, for this to be established.

Nearly two years after Geoffrey Burton's first production came that of Alan Gayton, who was to share with him the position of *primus inter pares* among the Society's producers for many years and to reintroduce pantomime as a regular feature of our programmes. His debut was with Frank Harvey's *The Poltergeist,* and it was a notable one. This play was rather lighter fare than the Society was accustomed to present at the time, but it was a farce of real quality greatly enjoyed by the audience and by those taking part.

Offstage this period in which the Society re-established itself after the war showed many interesting developments. The voucher system contined to be successful, and has been going ever since. The membership continued to rise. A feature of the social life which was very popular at the time, but which has had fluctuating fortunes since, was the tea-time canteen in the Clubroom. Actors and actresses, back-stage helpers and other willing members provided the voluntary and quite hard-worked staff on a rota basis. They were organised first by Renee Pochin, the Secretary's wife, and later by Edith Watson. The menu was considerably limited by post-war rationing, which for some time prevented the supplying of coffee to audiences, but the canteen was a cheerful and useful institution. It was complemented, in the days when there was no Theatre bar, by The Dover Castle across the road. At six o'clock many members made the transition from one to the other as regularly and automatically as a commuter changes to a train on the opposite platform.

And, of course, more fund raising was necessary. There was a very successful bazaar at the Edward Wood Hall, known as the Footlight Fair because its primary aim was to provide new lighting equipment. There were entertainments, including a good production of Fry's *A Phoenix Too Frequent* and a lively revue, *Bric-a-Brac*, mostly written by Peter Albrecht, who became a polished professional called Peter Arne. The profit on the venture was £1,328 11s. 2d.

In 1949 there had been a great stimulus to the actors and actresses of the Society in the form of a weekend course given by the Old Vic Drama School. I can remember, though not in any detail, a brilliantly witty lecture by John Blatchley in which he periodically punctuated his remarks with the phrase 'You know?'. At the time it seemed a charming affectation. We little knew that it was to spread from professional theatrical circles with the irresistible contagion of the Black Death to the English speaking public at large.

However, in other respects, the influence of Mr. Blatchley and his colleagues was wholly admirable. They gave us a most exciting weekend and insight into standards we should aspire to. The Old Vic came again in 1950, bringing a bonus in the lissom form of Litz Pisk, instructor in movement, dance and style, who talked – on Period Movement – as amusingly and fluently as the rest of the team and demonstrated a remarkable garment with voluminous folds that could be converted from a Roman toga to a pair of tights with a flick of the wrist – or so it seemed.

These experts also coaxed or bludgeoned out of a group of our members in a couple of hours a polished dressed-reading of a Chekhov farce which would have taken a couple of weeks of more pedestrian effort. In which of the two years this took place I wouldn't now care to say; but I have a clear general recollection of talented people being shown by brilliant people that they could stretch their powers and use them in a more exhilarating way than they had discovered before. I can't imagine that we could nowadays afford a group of instructors of comparable quality; but we were to repeat the experience in the sixties with equally inspiring results.

Sadly the early fifties saw the last of the Geoffrey Mead Shakespeare productions. These had appeared year after year in April as Birthday tributes, but, of course, the war had put an end to them. *Twelfth Night* had followed in 1947, and in 1951 it was decided that Geoffrey should produce one of the greatest Shakespeare tragedies, *King Lear*.

The King was played by Arthur Williams, a leading man of considerable stature with a fine, strong voice and a gift for conveying depth of feeling. He had taken part in many of the annual productions of the thirties, playing Hamlet in 1939. He gave a moving performance, well supported by a strong cast.

In the following year came Geoffrey's last production for the Society, and it was appropriate that it should be of a Shakespeare play, though of a less distinguished one, *The Merry Wives of Windsor*. This was his forty-sixth production, a number which has not yet been equalled by any other producer.

The twenty-first birthday of the Little Theatre was celebrated in 1951, with a production of *The Florentine Tragedy*, the one-act play by Oscar Wilde which had been performed on the night the Theatre was opened. It was produced by A. E. Christopherson, the only member of the Society in my memory whose christian name was never mentioned. His initials always appeared on the programme and he was known to everyone as Chris. He produced nine plays between 1944 and 1951, and had another claim to distinction, as being the only producer who could not, *and never tried to*, act. Nevertheless, he had a surprising knack of being able to show actors and actresses how to do so. The talent was, however, probably not much needed in dealing with Roy Pochin in the Wilde revival. Roy was playing the same part, Simone, which he had played twenty-one years before. Chris, who was a professional artist and art teacher, was also a superb set designer.

One cannot think of him without thinking also of his wife, Kathleen, who died in 1952 when she was only 47. They were a team, not in the sense that Kath always appeared in Chris's productions, but in the way they worked together in committee and in the social life of the Theatre towards the ends that they both hoped to achieve. They were great encouragers of young people in the Society, as I know from personal experience, and great advocates of new and creative ideas in the theatre.

Kathleen's obituary in the L.D.S. News Calendar speaks of her first playing in 1930 in *Loyalties* and of her many roles during the next twenty-two years. "She had", it says, "a ready wit, she was vivacious and good-looking and she brought all these qualities to whichever part she played."

Referring to the thirties: "During the same period, she and her husband (through the influence possibly of their training together at the Royal College of Art, where they first met) were pioneers in Leicester of a more non-commercial type of theatre – a theatre in which for the first time the influence of modern art began to be felt. *Aria de Capo* and *Orphée* by Cocteau were two productions in this genre which received considerable attention at the time. The former was described then as "a counterblast to comfortable thought" and through the whole of her comparatively short life, Kathleen Christopherson was the advocate, especially in the theatre, of new ideas and forms. It is a tribute to her and her husband that such things are now more easily acceptable in Dover Street than they were before."

Here then were two people who thought of drama primarily as an art form, and fortunately the L.D.S. has always had some such among its members, just as it has always had active members who leaned towards a theatre which was a less demanding place of light entertainment – and, of course, many who were happy with both kinds of theatre. The combination and interaction of all these has determined the Theatre's artistic policy; but another factor has always been the nature of the other stage entertainment available in the City at any given time.

In the thirties, as we have seen, the Drama Society could regard itself as the only consistent source of better quality drama in Leicester. At the time we are looking at now the same was still more or less the case. Immediately after the war the companies at the Theatre Royal were still pounding the exhausting threadmill of weekly rep., their output a generally unedifying stream of the most trivial comedies and thrillers, though they changed to a fortnightly regime in the early fifties with a consequent improvement in quality. Many West End successes appeared on tour either before or after their London run at the Opera House, which relieved the Drama Society of the necessity (or choice) of putting on plays which were entertaining enough as vehicles for star performers but which had little artistic merit.

Our own programme we find made up of classical revivals, revivals of more recent work, like that of Bridie, Priestley and Shaw, the plays of currently fashionable dramatists whose work was regarded as being of high quality, such as Fry, Ustinov, Rattigan and Anouilh, and, of course, a lot of middle-of-the-road plays which come into no particular category. Worthy enough material, generally speaking; but Geoffrey Burton, who wrote knowledgeably and perceptively about drama in the News Calendar during this period, speculated about whether we were quite carrying out our commitments as laid down when the Society was founded. Remarking on the fact that we had so far performed only one play by O'Casey, *Juno and the Paycock*, he looked for other gaps in our record:

> "After nearly thirty years we have produced only one Restoration play (*The Way of the World*), only one translation from Molière, and a mere three productions of Ibsen . . . We have yet to do a play by Strindberg, or by Eugene O'Neil or by Pirandello. Compare these to our twenty-three productions of plays by Bernard Shaw, nineteen of Old Will's, eleven of Galsworthy's and nine of J. B. Priestley's . . . Why we should neglect certain periods or playwrights I can't say but I wonder if Tyrone Guthrie is right when writing in this week's *Observer* he says, '. . . but when a committee chooses a work of art, the election invariably lights on what nobody minds rather than what anybody wants – the harmless rather than the excellent.' "

There is some truth in that, but I think an even more important factor was and is our attitude towards our audience, which we regard, rightly or wrongly, as intelligent but anti-intellectual, and as having little stomach for strong meat in the form of the too sad and too sordid – this would account for our neglect of Strindberg and O'Neil, which remains unrectified at the time of writing. Other gaps have been filled: Molière and Ibsen have had more or less their due; Pirandello has had a single showing; a second O'Casey, *The Plough and the Stars*, has been added; but fresh gaps have appeared in respect of contemporary dramatists, and these will be considered in their turn.

Returning to the 1950s, Christopher Fry was popular at this time. He is rather scorned at present, but was at least a witty and ingenious wordsmith. Burton produced *Venus Observed* and Gayton *The Lady's Not For Burning* and the casts included a number of players I am pleased to have the opportunity to mention. In the former Gilbert

Boys' Joy-Riding

"BOB" SEES HASSAN.

"BOB" AT THE OPENING OF THE LITTLE THEATRE

The opening of the Little Theatre and the first full-length production, as seen by the cartoonist "Bob" of the Leicester Evening Mail.

The set for the 1933 production of *Martine* reproduced from a nineteen-thirties book on the repertory theatre.

Harry Martin, Leslie Bowmar and William Box in *Yellow Sands* (1936).

Frank Tabberer and James Wheeler in Geoffrey Mead's play *Remember Sparta* (1938).

The cast of *Bird in Hand* (1941). Second from the left, back row, is Alan Gayton; Second from the right is Clifton James (Monty's double'). In the front row are Dora Tabberer and Walter Martin.

Moyra Haywood.

Gillard gave one of his most elegant performances as the Duke of Altair. He was a leading man of power and authority, the sort it is not easy to come by in an amateur society, one who had the accent and the bearing to play an arrogant aristocrat or an old-style Tory prime minister with conviction. Among the ladies were Brenda Burrows, Nina Goodman and Patricia Wilkie, all actresses of good looks and distinction.

In *The Lady's Not For Burning* the central character, Thomas Mendip, was played by Laurence Neal, who took many leading parts during the twenty-odd years after the war. He could always be relied on for a highly intelligent interpretation of character and meticulous pointing of lines, and had a fine and infectious sense of humour. He was also a regular producer. The two brothers in the play were played by Philip Berridge, who was a first choice juvenile lead for several years, and Henry Livings, who did some useful work for the L.D.S. before turning professional, first at the Theatre Royal and later in his native North Country, where he resumed his original accent and became a successful dramatist. The leading lady was again Brenda Burrows, and the part of Tappercoom, made notable in the professional theatre by the booming Peter Bull, was played by Robert Martin, son of Harry Martin, himself the possessor of a fine deep voice and much in demand for leading roles.

Arthur Williams was now reaching the end of his career with the Society. He played Capulet in the 1952 production of *Romeo and Juliet*. He gave his usual strong performance, but was by now, like so many older actors and actresses, beginning to have a little trouble with remembering lines, a fact which gave rise to the story, undoubtedly apochryphal, that whenever he dried up he would cry, "Torches before me! Ho!" and sweep off the stage with his entourage.

Walter Martin, one of the three original founders of the Society, died in 1952. He had played his last part in the Theatre, the Judge in *Winterset*, the year before, under the direction of his nephew, Robert. His services to the L.D.S. had been invaluable, but he had also been for several years a professional actor, and his method was unique, as the words of Geoffrey Burton, writing his obituary for the News Calendar, make clear:

"Walter Martin was essentially an Actor – using the word in the old-fashioned sense – and he had little time for the modern

Producer's Theatre. He was a past master at his craft, especially in comedy, where his timing showed a technique rarely to be seen off the professional stage . . . Each part he played was most carefully considered and his Acting-Copy was always marked with the most elaborate instructions detailing where he was going to take a breath, raise his eyebrows, take off his glasses, etc., with the result that his performances were strictly controlled in the Coquelin manner rather than individual creations. He believed in the maximum of effect and with the sort of temperament invariably found in great artists, this led him into various tussles with producers – particularly when he was being directed by his brother . . ."

I remember the glee with which Walter devised his favourite piece of business when he played the Judge in *Toad of Toad Hall*, shaping a bit of nose putty and sticking a quill pen in it, so that he could belance it on his nose during the Trial Scene. I remember too the generosity of his praise for other, and especially for younger, actors. "Splendid performance!" he would say, "Never seen the part played so well!" How warming such words were coming from one so experienced and so accomplished. And if the effect of dear Walter's encouragement was a little diluted when one came to realise that he said much the same sort of thing to nearly everyone else, one never doubted his sincerity or good will.

1953 was Coronation Year. This was not of great significance to the theatre, except that on the great day itself (in June, it will be remembered) a large number of loyal actors and actresses took part in a municipal procession which progressed slowly from Victoria Park to Abbey Park through heavy rain. Most were dressed as Shakespearean characters, and my wife, Pauline, was perched high on a dais on a float impersonating the Virgin Queen. The gracious smile with which she acknowledged the cheers of the crowd and the cries of "Good old Liz!" became gradually more fixed and insincere as her face became streaked with red hair dye and a small pond settled on her stomach because her tight Elizabethan waist refused to release the water admitted at chest level. It was very cold. Her ladies in waiting suffered equally and the pedestrians only less in that the motion of their legs, though cased in clammy tights, generated a modicum of warmth. Loyalty was strained. In the theatre the evening performance of a not wholly successful production of *Man and Superman* played to about twenty-seven people. Not the most glorious of days.

These were disastrous times for theatre in Leicester. The Opera House had closed in May 1952 and by September 1953 it was up for auction with the condition of sale that it must not be used as a theatre again. It was remembered in Dover Street as the place where our own earliest productions had been staged. The sale did not take place, and the condition must have been withdrawn, for in 1955 the Secretary received a letter from Prince Littler offering to sell the building to the L.D.S. But it was never re-opened and was finally demolished. The Theatre Royal was also on its last legs, and in September 1954 at the A.G.M. of the Drama Society the Treasurer, Geoffrey Hilton, was telling the meeting, "our Theatre, in the absence of professional theatres in the city, has a great responsibility to Leicester". Our own attendances had not been satisfactory and he stressed the need to attract more voucher holders.

This was in spite of some particularly good productions, including a thoughtful and moving *The Three Sisters* by Geoffrey Burton, immediately followed by Fry's adaptation of Anouilh's *Ring Round the Moon* produced by Alan Gayton, which was the only play to take over £300 that season. The latter was notable for a superb set, painted by George Kelman, which featured a fountain with real water, and for a splendid fight between two of the Society's most attractive and talented ladies, Ruth Elliott and Margaret Faulkner.

Christmas shows at this time always presented a problem: that of what to fill in the gaps with until we could decently put on *Treasure Island* or *Toad of Toad Hall* again. But in the 54/55 season it was again the turn of *Treasure Island*, the one and only (though not unsuccessful) production of Frank Srawley. This is especially remembered for the occasion when the cannon, represented by a magnificently deafening and set-shattering explosion which the Fire Department would hardly allow nowadays, went off a quarter of an hour too soon. Victor Bonfield, as Captain Smollett, played a captain's part by striding on to the deck and announcing that the Squire's tobacco had just exploded in the powder magazine.

Just before this in November yet another Footlight Fair had been held to bolster our rather meagre financial resources and provide the means to make improvements to the foyer. One novel feature of this Fair was a film by Douglas Goodlad of the activities of the Society, entitled *Half an Hour, Please*, lasting just about that long, and incorporating illustrative shots of seven of the more recent L.D.S. productions. As it turned out, the record contained in this film of features of the stage and the dressing-rooms was even more important than Douglas had supposed, since much of what he filmed was shortly to be changed or obliterated by the fire.

Before we turn to that most dramatic of incidents in the history of the Theatre, one more show should be mentioned. Early in 1955 Geoffrey Burton produced Obey's *Noah*. This was impressive for the set and the props (there were some striking animals' heads), but most of all for the performance of Roy Pochin in the title role. This was one of Roy's last appearances and it must surely have been one of his finest characterisations. It was humorous and urbane (after the manner of the man who played it) and it was deeply moving without ever descending to sentimentality.

One social event must also be recorded: the first Theatre Ball, which took place in January at the Grand Hotel. The President, now Geoffrey Mead, received the guests with his wife, Kathleen. The Lord Mayor came with the Lady Mayoress, and though the event was thought to be rather highly priced at 15/- (75p.) it was so generally enjoyed that it was determined to repeat it the following year. This was done, and there has been a Ball almost every year since, most of them notable, as becomes a Society like the L.D.S., for a particularly high standard of cabaret entertainment.

CHAPTER 6

The Fire and its Consequences

Early in April 1955 Robert Martin and Alan Gayton jointly produced *The Love of Four Colonels* – a successful production with a very
strong cast. When the set was struck, its place was taken by that of
Lilac Time, which was being staged by the newly-formed Leicester
Operatic Ensemble and produced by Lilian Dunkley. This played to
full houses for three nights, but when the theatre was locked for the
night at the end of the third an unwelcome visitor was left inside. I
quote the Leicester Mercury for the 21st April:

"Leicester's Little Theatre, home of the Leicester Drama Society,
was severely damaged early today in a blaze which destroyed the
stage, dressing rooms, and most of the rear of the building.

"This morning there was a gaping hole in the roof and the building
flooded with water from fireman's hoses . . .

"When the fire was at its worst a figure of a man was seen to crawl
on to the roof of the neighbouring footwear factory of Briggs
Industrial Footwear, Ltd. and he had to be rescued by an escape
ladder. A man was later detained by the police and taken to the
Leicester Police Headquarters.

"Later Edward Michael Harrison Owen (31), Portman Street,
Leicester, appeared in court and was remanded in custody until
tomorrow, charged with stealing a quantity of imitation jewellery,
a stage revolver, 37 cartridges and other articles, together valued
at £15, from Leicester Drama Society, Ltd.

"The fire was spotted shortly after one o'clock this morning by
Police Constable A. Iliffe on beat duty.

"The alarm was raised and when the fire brigade arrived flames
were leaping through the roof at the rear of the premises.

"At one stage it looked as if the fire was getting out of control and
reinforcements were called for.

"Briggs' footwear factory was threatened and also Browett's garage
in Dover Street, and the Dover Castle public house.

"Mrs. Florence Thorley, wife of the licensee of the Dover Castle,
told a reporter: 'When the police told us about the fire, I looked

out of my bedroom window and saw a man on the roof of Briggs' factory.

" 'He was clinging to a telegraph pole and seemed to be swaying. I thought he was going to fall, but the fire brigade rescued him.' "

A less reliable report avers that the man was taken across to the Dover, and when Mrs. Thorley, a warm friend of the Theatre, which provided good custom in those days, realised that the glass of brandy she had been asked to bring was intended for the exhausted male-factor, she cried, "That booger 'ent 'avin' it!", and, in the traditional gesture of theatrical farce, drained the glass herself.

Next morning the news soon got round, and officers and committee members wandered disconsolately among blackened timbers and sodden débris trying to calculate the extent of the damage. It turned out that the stage, the dressing rooms, and the greater part of the scenery, properties and wardrobe had been virtually destroyed and the clubroom damaged; but that the auditorium and the Moyra Haywood Hall below it had escaped. It was at once decided that we should carry on, and Pauline Graham, the producer of the play currently in rehearsal, *To Live in Peace*, was asked if she could stage it downstairs instead of in the theatre.

The May edition of the News Calendar, now edited by Leslie Walker, was hurried out, and it contained a message from Geoffrey Mead, the President:

"Our testing time", he wrote, "will lie in the weeks and months ahead, when the fun of improvisation begins to pall, and the difficulties of putting on a show, without all those hundred and one ready to hand aids which we have come to take for granted, become more apparent.

"It is then that every member of this Society of ours will meet a challenge of his or her sincerity and loyalty, and I am confident that this challenge will gladly be accepted by all . . .

"And now a word as to the future. Time may well show that the fire, which has curtailed our work and consumed so many treasures in its fury, will prove a blessing in disguise; and that from the tragic sight of ruin, and ashes, and muck, and disorder, will arise a backstage layout in which better work than ever can be done, under easier conditions than were possible in the badly designed building which has been so battered and bent."

And this prophecy was to prove a true one.

Meanwile, rehearsals for *To Live in Peace* went on. One took place on the Sunday after the fire in the clubroom, which was thought to be safe, until someone glanced up towards the ceiling and noticed the large globular lampshades two-thirds full of water, like so many pendant goldfish bowls.

Other rehearsals took place at Vaughan College, home of the Vaughan Players, for many years the friendliest of rival drama societies, where the authorities generously found room for us to rehearse and also to hold members' evenings.

In the Theatre willing volunteers worked furiously to turn the Moyra Haywood Hall into a theatre.

There was already a stage of sorts at one end, and the Hall was twice as large as it is now because it still contained the section which has since become the bar. But, as the Honorary Secretary said in a programme note: "Much has had to be done at short notice – the stage enlarged, new scenery made and painted, lighting equipment begged or hired and fixed in position, seating to be planned and battened together and finally new dressing rooms to be built". All the moves for the play had to be changed too, since the stage was much smaller and the entrances more limited. Nevertheless the show opened on May 9th, eighteen days after the fire.

The 'dressing rooms' took the form of a long narrow strip at the side of the hall further from Dover Street, which was separated from the audience only by a hardboard partition, so that during the performance the players who occupied it had to observe a monastic silence. The graveyard, a survival from the Baptist chapel days, which the theatre buildings enclosed, served them as greenroom in fine weather and occasionally as emergency lavatory. But many of the productions in the makeshift theatre were as successful as any we have done, and the very limitations imposed on staging seemed to stimulate the imagination and inventiveness of producers. Audiences, while exercising as always their right to stay away from shows they didn't fancy, remained generally loyal, and the Society kept going cheerfully and hopefully until January 1958, when the new theatre was ready.

Work on the new theatre was begun as soon as possible. Of course, special committees were set up: the Re-Building Committee, to deal with problems of design and equipment; and the Appeals Committee, to set about, on an even bigger scale than usual, the ever-recurring task of raising money.

Alan Gayton was, more than any other single person, responsible for the planning of the new stage and back-stage, though he was strongly supported by Geoffrey Burton and Frank Cooper Watson, an architect by profession and an invaluable technical adviser. Hardly a year after the fire, Alan was showing members an excellent model of the theatre as it was to be, the most exciting feature of which was a large removable forestage which would enable the action of plays to be brought forward in front of the proscenium arch. (If the fire had been a few years later, the design would probably not have shown a proscenium arch at all.) In July 1956 the Council accepted a tender from Mesrs. A. E. Cox and Co. to carry out the re-building.

The Restoration Fund was, of course, needed to ensure that the new theatre would be much better than the old one, rather than to pay for the basic structure, for the Council had seen to it that the insurance cover was adequate – it included, for instance, consequential loss of revenue.

To make the desired improvement possible the Appeals Committee, which comprised the Council and representatives of General Committee, set themselves a target of £10,000. Since the Society had manifestly suffered a major misfortune, the appeal had a head start over some fund-raising efforts and met with a sympathetic response. In 1956, for example, the Leicester Association of Musical Societies handed over £500 which it had raised, largely by a special production of *Rose Marie* at the De Montfort Hall. A number of generous donations – including one of £1,000 by Mr. Percy Gee – were received from individuals and businesses.

The closure of the Theatre Royal, which left the Little as the only remaining live theatre, while deeply deplored, provided the Society with a considerable quantity of scenery at bargain prices. About five pantechnicon- and two lorry-loads of flats, rostrums, reveal doors and sundries were purchased for £65. But still the specifications were having to be scrutinised to see what economies – such as cheaper facing bricks on the street frontage and concrete instead of terrazzo floors in the lavatories – could be effected to bring the costs of re-building within the means likely to be available. Hundreds of pounds were saved by working parties of members carrying out jobs which would otherwise have had to be done professionally.

The peak of the fund-raising was a special effort called, predictably, the Phoenix Fair, held in the Edward Wood Hall from the 28th to the 30th of November, 1957. There were all the usual stalls, a revue and a new film by Douglas Goodlad called *In Such a Night*, which featured the fire. The Society was particularly indebted to the two famous openers, David Kossoff and Jack Hulbert, who did not charge for their admirable services. The target of £3,000 was exceeded.

There were, of course many problems and setbacks. The scheduled completion date for the new theatre had been August 19th 1957, but because of delays caused by sub-contractors this had to be pushed forward more than three months, leaving an uncomfortably short time for the preparations which must precede the opening in the following January.

But it was generally felt that the period of hard work and discomfort which now was coming to an end had also been one of commendable achievement. In his Secretary's report to the Council in August 1957 Roy Pochin was able to say, "I think we can safely claim that during the past season our standard of production has been well maintained . . . In spite of uncomfortable seating, bad ventilation and poor visibility, our audiences have kept up well in numbers, showing that in Leicester there is a small, but loyal, following for the live theatre which should be capable of expansion when we return to the theatre proper . . . I should like to place on record my appreciation of the work of the staff, particularly Mr. Julian, who has worked untiringly under most adverse and even unhealthy conditions . . ."

Poor Fred had had to move out of his office, which was being rebuilt, and for some time held court in the foyer, which, had had £1,000 spent on it not long before the fire, but was not equipped for its new purpose or adequately heated. But the Manager spent his days there, grumbling happily, overcoated and scarved in winter, and always supplied with Beecham's Powder, a preparation in which he had implicit faith, dispensing it generously to anyone who seemed to need.

By December everything essential was finished, and the ambition to build a better theatre than the one which had been partially destroyed had been fulfilled. Apart from the new forestage, which had separate entrances to right and left of it, and which could be replaced by an orchestra pit for musicals, the biggest gain was perhaps the new lighting box, situated at the back of the auditorium, so that the technicians could operate in response to visual cues as well as those received from the stage manager through the inter-comm. There was a much better lighting board than we had had before, with plenty of scope for adding to its efficiency when more money was available.

New storage space for flats and rostrums had been provided on the ground floor, with easier access from the street, and a hoist had been installed to lift them up to the back stage area. Here an enormous double door had been put in, like something in a giraffe's enclosure, so that full-sized flats could be pushed directly into the wings.

By amateur theatrical standards – and some professional, I believe – the dressing room accommodation, not inadequate before, was palatial; no separate rooms for stars, certainly, but an individual place with a chair and a mirror with a lamp on either side of it for a cast of up to forty. The old props room had become a dressing room, and a mezzanine floor, between the ground floor and the stage itself, had been provided for props and scenery.

The Moyra Haywood Hall was now available for rehearsal again and the clubroom, though somewhat curtailed to make room for a new wardrobe room on the ground floor, was still large enough to give a rehearsal area more or less equivalent to the size of the stage upstairs.

As in 1930 the Committee looked for a first play which was something of a spectacular, with a large cast, presenting opportunities to show off to the full the resources of the stage and the lighting board. They chose *Tiger at the Gates* by Jean Giraudoux, in the translation of Christopher Fry. Entitled *La Guerre de Troie n'aura pas lieu* in the 1935 original, it was a lively and stylish discussion play dealing with the attempts of Priam, Hector, Ulysses, Ajax and the rest to avert the Trojan War, which invited analogy with the problems of war and the causes of war in the modern world. Like a historical play by Shaw, it was leavened with humour, and even gave us a chance to show that the fly-rail was still working by introducing a goddess, Iris, on a cloud, to contribute to the debate. This led to one of those rare and memorable mishaps; for one night a stage hand let a controlling rope slip, and, instead of being lowered vertically on her lofty perch, the goddess was swung in like a pendulum. Understandably enough, her words deserted her. She had a sizeable speech and was suspended high above the stage, far beyond the reach of the prompter's life-belt. She struggled manfully – if a goddess can – continuing to utter, but with no claim to coherence, for what seemed a fearfully long time, until Priam was inspired to cry, "Thank you, Iris!", the cue to the stage management for her removal.

The play was produced by Geoffrey Burton, the Chairman of the Society, with Alan Gayton as his stage director and set designer. Priam and Hector were played by Gilbert Gillard and James Wheeler, and Ajax and Ulysses by Philip Berridge and Robert Martin.

The set, painted by George Kelman, was impressive; and it may be noted here that the theatre has always had a high reputation for the quality of its scenery. Since the thirties a professional scenic artist has been employed, and for most of the time, until his retirement in 1974, it was George Kelman, whose skill cannot be too highly praised. He would design a set if the producer wanted him to, or if the producer presented him with a design to follow he would reproduce it in meticulous detail even if he did not entirely approve of it. He might grumble a bit, and sometimes would tell a producer that what he asked for could not be done – and as often as not the producer would arrive the next day to find that it had been done. He was a fine craftsman who took pride in his craft, and he did much to enhance the theatre's reputation.

It took some producers a little while to learn how to make the best possible use of the resources which were now at their disposal, and, of course, there were disappointing shows as well as artistically satisfying ones; but everyone had it in mind to try to make the productions approach as nearly as possible to those of the professional theatre, allowing an adequate rehearsal period, expecting dress rehearsals to be polished and ready, and using well-organised teams of props, lighting and other back-stage work.

In 1955 Geoffrey Burton had become Chairman of Committee in succession to Frank Gayton, and in 1958 Roy Pochin, having served as Honorary Secretary for fourteen years and seen through the rebuilding of the Theatre, resigned from that office, and was succeeded by Alan Gayton. So began a partnership of chairman and secretary which was to last for ten years, a period of stability in the leadership of the Society which was to consolidate the work put in on the planning and construction of the new building and to bring about many improvements.

CHAPTER 7

New Ideas, On and Off Stage

During the middle and late fifties, which was a period of such excitement and change for the Little Theatre, a revolution was also taking place in the larger world of the Drama. The twenties, thirties and forties had been a time of very humdrum writing in the English theatre. The only great dramatists at work in Britain were the Irishmen, Shaw and O'Casey. In the search for modern plays of more than usual interest and significance we had had to turn frequently to America or to France, as in the case of the play chosen to open the re-built Theatre. The serious student of Drama looking for English material could find only the poetical plays of Eliot and Fry, with the possibility that Rattigan might prove to be a dramatist whose work was of lasting merit.

The breakthrough, which saw English writers freeing themselves from the bonds of convention and producing work which was at least fresh, stimulating and controversial, came with the production in 1956 of John Osborne's *Look Back in Anger*, and continued with work by, among others, Pinter, Wesker and John Arden.

This work posed something of a problem to a theatre like ours, as it did to the commercial theatre. Though each of the writers mentioned had his own individual style and evoked a unique response, they had this in common: that they made greater demands on audiences than dramatists who only sought to entertain with a good story; they asked for a more positive emotional or intellectual involvement and reaction; they presented to the audience aspects of life which had not commonly been shown before in the English Theatre.

The problem was, of course, that a proportion of the Little Theatre's customers, like those in other theatres, much preferred to sit back and passively enjoy a good story. They came to the theatre to be entertained, not to be made to feel guilty. They knew that snotty-nosed old men spat and swore, but were unwilling to pay good money to watch them doing it.

The phrase 'kitchen-sink drama' was coined, and, like all terms of blanket condemnation, often invoked unjustly. The dilemma was that the 'new' dramatists were on the whole more lively and original in their use of language, more perceptive and probing in their presentation of character, and certainly more thought-provoking than the old. So many producers and actors wanted to work on their plays and a certain section of the audience wanted to see them. But to many they were offensive and to others comparatively uninteresting because the story element in their work was less important than it had been in the case of more conventional playwrights.

This difficulty has been with us since 1956. Since that time many of our most brilliant and stylish writers have turned out plays which could only appeal to a minority audience. They have seemed too important to neglect, but too unpopular to run many box-office risks with.

Characteristically, the L.D.S. has generally met this problem in a spirit of compromise, slipping a controversial work into the pro-gramme as often as it dared, sometimes with surprisingly successful, sometimes with unfortunate, results. *Look Back in Anger* was produced, by Douglas Goodlad, in 1959, only three years after it had startled the play-going public at the Royal Court. The 'only' is not meant ironically, because for any new play there is always a time-lag for amateurs, who have to wait for the rights until the professionals have finished with it, and there is another interval of some months between a play's being chosen by committee and actually presented.

It played to quite good houses and the audience on the whole responded favourably to the dramatic impact of Osborne's powerful invective, given a strong performance by a good cast led by Tony Ward as Jimmy Porter. Earlier in the year there had been another successful production of a serious and thought-provoking play. This was Arthur Miller's *Death of a Salesman*, which seemed an ambitious choice for us, calling on a large cast to acquire American accents and dealing critically with a way of life which was then not quite so familiar as it is now. But the meticulous care of Geoffrey Burton's production and the obvious sincerity of the writing and acting called forth the right emotional response.

But the most popular success of the year 1959 was Alan Gayton's production of Benn W. Levy's *The Rape of the Belt*. Sincerity is the quality which the amateur theatre can most easily achieve; but this presentation of a delightfully artificial comedy proved that it can on occasion achieve elegance and style.

Sometimes a play which has caused no great stir elsewhere may turn out to be ideal for a Little Theatre. This was the case with *The Offshore Island*, Marghanita Laski's play about a handful of survivors from a nuclear holocaust, which was only the second production (1960) of Neville Williams and showed the sensitive treatment of a moving story which was also to be a feature of much of his later work. The leading lady was Pauline Graham.

Pauline had the daunting, but exciting, task in the following year of producing *Waiting for Godot*. This controversial play, which some considered the poetic creation of a genius and others the pretentious ramblings of a charlatan, had been splitting committees on and off for a year or two, and had previously been scheduled for production and withdrawn. Now it was at last put on, and was quite well attended. Though there was the usual handful of customers who did not come back after the interval that we get when we present a play which outrages the conservative, it was greeted as a success by those who hold it to be a great play of the sort the L.D.S. should not shy away from, and also by many who came to sneer and stayed at least to applaud politely.

The year 1961 was saddened by the death of Roy Pochin, whose last office had been that of President. Enough has been written already about him to indicate what a keystone he had been to the Society from the very beginning. No member can have been better loved. Albert Northfold, his old friend and successor as President, ended his tribute to Roy in the News Calendar:

"Numerous and varied were the exceptional talents with which Roy was endowed, and which he used unsparingly for the good of others. Yet to his friends, the qualities that will be longest remembered will be his unvarying courtesy and graciousness.

"We shall all miss him, but will surely offer up a prayer of thankfulness for the privilege of having had him in our midst."

This was the year too of the retirement of Fred Julian after sixteen years of dedicated service as Manager. He was succeeded by Michael Cocks, a kind and helpful man, devoted to the Theatre, who was incredibly to prove as unstinting of his time as Fred had been.

A notable innovation was the creation of Heads of Departments backstage. The backstage work of the Society had never been less than efficient, but now it was felt that the service to producers could be made even more so by the appointment of a Senior Stage Manager to oversee all productions and to appoint a stage manager to each one, and by similar appointments to superintend Lighting, Properties, Wardrobe and Prompting. A producer could now choose his own backstage personnel if he wished, or he could ask the head of the appropriate department to suggest a suitable person to him. There were some misgivings at first that the system might lead to too much specialisation, but it worked well on the whole, saving producers a lot of worry and ensuring a uniformly high standard of backstage work. The first of the S.S.M.s was Jack Roberts, who got the scheme off to a splendid start; and when he was forced to relinquish the post Nigel Pochin, Roy's son, an experienced and accomplished S.M., took over.

The outstanding production of 1962, and something of a landmark in the Theatre's artistic history, was Alan Gayton's *Julius Caesar*. The practice of doing an annual Shakespeare had died out, and Shakespeare had been presented only occasionally, since it was often felt that our male acting strength was too weak to do the great playwright justice. But now *Caesar* was chosen, and in the important parts of Cassius and Antony the producer cast two young men who were new to the Society. They were Martin Caven and John Ghent; and Brutus was played by the seasoned and mellifluous James Wheeler. The set was original and exciting, the standard of verse-speaking was unusually high and the crowd work was excellent. This success led to a series of good Shakespearean productions, several of which were the work of the same John Ghent. As for Martin Caven, no actor contributed more outstanding performances during the years which followed.

Another production from the same season which is still remembered was that by Laurence Neal of Brendan Behan's *The Hostage*, the story of a young English soldier held and finally shot by the I.R.A. in a sleazy brothel. Any misgivings that the audiences might have felt about the unpleasantness of the setting and subject matter were soon dispelled by the vigorous originality of the language, the richly varied characterisation and a blending of comedy and pathos which recalled O'Casey. These virtues were successfully brought out by a well-paced production and some fine acting.

Successes like these keep a drama society in good heart, but the occasional failures rankle, and the need to work hard at keeping standards of production and acting consistently high can never be lost sight of. Remembering the stimulus which has been given by the visit of the Old Vic School, the Productions Committee looked for another source of inspiration through professional instruction, and found it, in September 1962, by inviting Harold Lang of the Central School of Speech and Drama to visit us for a week-end with his colleagues Nicholas Amer and Greville Hallam. Mary Angrave, the chairman of the committee, worked very hard at organising this visit, which was of immense value. Harold Lang was a brilliant teacher who communicated not only enthusiasm but a memorable theory of the technique of acting which made a lasting impression on those who assimilated it. The principles he laid down in his opening lecture on the Action on the Stage are worth repeating. His creed was that the actor should ask himself certain questions about the character he is playing in any given stage situation:

1. What does he (or she) want?
2. What are they trying to do to get it?
3. To whom or what are they doing it?
4. By what means?
5. Against what resistance?
6. In order to, what?

Richard III (1949). Leslie Walker as Richmond and David Lyall as Richard.

Ring Round the Moon (1954).

To Live in Peace (1955), the first play to be produced on the stage in the Moyra Haywood Hall after the fire.

Tiger at the Gates (1958), the first play to be produced in the rebuilt theatre.

The Rebuilding of the Little Theatre

Architects

FRANK BROWN & A. L. SHARPE, *Chartered Architects*

Main Contractors

A. E. COX & CO. (Builders) LTD.

Sub-contractors

Steelwork — S. RUSSELL & SON LTD.   *Electrical and Gas Installation* — F. WEBB & SON.

Heating Engineers — YOUNG, AUSTEN & YOUNG LTD.   *Plumbing* — WILLIAM FREER LTD.

Wood block floors — HOLLIS BROS. LTD.   *Asphalting* — FLEXIMASTIC LTD.   *Stage Lighting* —

STRAND ELECTRIC & ENGINEERING CO. LTD.   *Stage Equipment* — HALL STAGE EQUIPMENT LTD.

Decorating Auditorium — A. E. COX & CO. LTD.   *Decorating Foyer* — ARTHUR HART & SON

Seating & Carpeting — BECK & WINDIBANK LTD.

The Auditorium decor and the mural panels by A. E. CHRISTOPHERSON, ESQ.

Rebuilding
Committee
of the
Leicester
Drama Society

Frank Gayton (Chairman)   *Alan Gayton (Secretary)*   *Frank Cooper Watson*   *Geoffrey Burton*

Frank Wincett   *H. Roy Pochin*   *J. Geoffrey Hilton*   *Geoffrey W. Mead*   *R. Eric Pochin*

A page from the programme of *Tiger at the Gates*, giving credit to those responsible for the rebuilding.

The Rape of the Belt (1959), with Robert Martin coming through the wall.

Julius Caesar (1962), with Gilbert Gillard standing centre and James Wheeler on the right.

It sound fairly obvious, I suppose, but it had people concentrating as never before.

The lecture was followed by a practical class in physical/ psychological exercises, and the Sunday sessions were taken up with detailed and comprehensive practical work on a scene from *Macbeth*.

During this course Harold Lang became not only an inspiration to the Society, but also a friend; so much so that he did us the great honour of allowing us to stage his performance, in January 1963, of the world première of his dramatic lecture, *Macbeth in Camera*, which was so impressive that the British Council sent it on a tour of the Americas. There followed a succession of letters between Mary Angrave and Lang to and from all sorts of exotic places which led to a further course for L.D.S. members in October 1963, continuing the work of the previous year and adding valuable sessions on "How to Set Up an Improvisation" and "Making Speech Expressive".

That October also saw the opening of the Phoenix Theatre. So we happily ceased to be the only representatives of live theatre in Leicester. A number of our members, notably Geoffrey Burton and Alan Gayton, were associated with the venture in an advisory capacity, and we soon made another professional friend in Clive Perry, the director of the new theatre. He took a kind and flattering interest in our work and later (in 1965) directed two plays for us, *The Marriage-Go-Round* and *War and Peace*.

Perry's methods led to some controversy in our Society. It was his practice to let actors and actresses evolve their own moves during the course of rehearsal, whereas it was usual for our producers to plan and plot all moves before the first rehearsals, during which the players were told these moves and wrote them down. Some of our producers were keen to keep up with the latest ideas in the theatre, and were persuaded by Perry's argument that the actor was entitled to give expression to his interpretation of character in movement as well as in speech and gesture, and that the result of his doing so was likely to be more natural than if he were mechanically going into positions laid down for him by the producer. Others held that the interaction of two or more characters had to be directed by the producer, and that in any case the Perry method, employed with amateur actors, would waste too much of our limited and valuable rehearsal time. Geoffrey Burton put the modern theory into practice in his later productions, but it is impossible to tell how different the end product was from what it would otherwise have been. Other producers may perhaps have been more willing now to modify the moves that they had planned as a result of ideas brought forward by the actors. It would, I think, be fair to say that most actors preferred to be told where to go and to do their interpreting from then on. Certainly most producers now seem to have reverted to the older practice.

Having a stage and equipment in the new theatre which was more or less what we wanted, the Committee turned its attention to the other end of the building, where the foyer, having been undamaged by the fire, remained unimproved. Under the leadership of Alan Gayton the plan to give the Theatre a foyer worthy of the new stage, to be known as Project F, and inevitably, backed by a Foyer Fund, was launched in 1963.

The change was badly needed. The way up to the theatre auditorium was by two straight and narrow staircases in the wall to the right of the entrance, roughly where the two doors to the bar now are. The box-office was between them. These stairs were a trial to the elderly and the unfit, made the filling and emptying of the auditorium a slow business, and nowadays would certainly be considered dangerous. The plan was to build a first-floor extension over the old foyer, to which a new and wider and less steep staircase would lead. From the newly created upstairs foyer, extensive enough to have room for a confectionery counter and a men's lavatory and to afford wall space for exhibitions, the audience would be led by two doorways into the theatre. This plan was presented in the 1963 A.G.M., but it was an expensive one and its completion seemed a long way off. However, it was finally achieved in 1967.

During this period of the early and middle sixties the Theatre was again experiencing financial difficulties – not the sort of edge-of-cliff crisis which had threatened its existence in the thirties, but a worrying shortage of funds brought about by disappointing attendance at the plays. A special budgetary sub-committee was set up.

The first thing that happened to alleviate the situation was the Christmas show of the 1963/4 season, when, after many years, the tradition of an annual pantomime was re-introduced. When the idea was mooted a group of members got together to discuss how this could best be done, and the result was the production by Alan

Gayton of *Puss in Boots*, using a script obtained from Northampton Rep. With excellent singers – Olwen Kershaw and Julia Byham – as principal boy and girl and a lovable dame from Frank Choice, this was a great success, and it was subsequently found that pantomime would play to full houses for three weeks or more, thus subsidising a number of less popular productions. Most of the shows since the first have been written by members, the majority being contributed by Thea Craine.

Looking forward a few years to 1968 we find the pantomime being supplemented as a major regular source of revenue by the annual Old Time Music Hall. The man responsible for this second money-spinning innovation was Geoffrey Sharp, who came to the L.D.S. from London bringing many valuable ideas from his theatre there. The Music Hall was put on at his suggestion; he produced it; and to most people's surprise the demand for it continued year after year. It has always run for two weeks or more, filling all the seats except those left empty to facilitate the sale of alcoholic beverages to the audience.

These measures helped considerably to solve the problem of showing a profit on a season's productions and maintaining the steady flow of cash which is needed to keep a hundred-years-old building from falling apart. In addition special fund-raising aimed to attract audiences by improving the Theatre's appearance and amenities. To this end Project F beavered away during 1964, culminating in a Motley Market in November which was opened on the two days when it took place by Jack Train and Norman Hartnell, and which raised nearly £3,000.

To make the outlook brighter still, at the end of the 1965 A.G.M. the Hon. Secretary (still Alan Gayton) surprised his audience by reading an announcement from a late edition of the *Mercury*. It read:

"The City Council's General Purposes Committee is to recommend that an interest-free loan of £12,000 be made to Leicester Drama Society Limited.

"In a statement the Chairman of the Committee, Sir Mark Henig, says: 'The Committee recognise the excellent work done by the Society since its formation in the 1920's and the pleasure and entertainment it has given to the people of Leicester and the surrounding areas for the past 35 years since it acquired the Little Theatre, in Dover Street.

"'After the fire in the theatre in 1958 (sic), the society rebuilt and refurnished the stage, workshops, dressing rooms and much of the downstairs accommodation, at a cost of £36,000.

"'The auditorium (which was not burned) is in good condition but the exterior of the old part of the building badly needs restoration and there is a great need for improvements in "Front of House" to provide better audience facilities.

"'There is a particular need for a new and larger foyer with easier stairs up to the auditorium and a bar, for which a provisional licence has been granted.

"'The General Purposes Committee has decided therefore to make an interest-free loan of £12,000 to the Society to facilitate the carrying out of these improvements. The loan will be repayable over a period of 20 years.

"'The General Purposes Committee has every confidence in Leicester Drama Society and believes that this assistance will not only improve the facilities enjoyed by audiences at the theatre, but will also enable the Society to make the greatest use of its most valuable asset and so strengthen its financial position.'"

One other measure announced that year, which was designed to improve attendances at shows, was a rather desperate one: to reduce the number of shows to ten and run them for two weeks. This didn't work and didn't last. By 1969 we had reached the pattern which prevails at the time of writing – of ten straight plays (occasionally a musical among them) with the annual pantomime (or other Christmas attraction) and Music Hall in addition. If any show seemed likely to justify a run of ten days or more it has been given it, but the normal run for a play has been one week.

Another decision reached in 1965 and mentioned by Sir Mark was of vital importance to the future of the Theatre: that a bar should be installed. It had for many years been a point of contention in committee and Council whether this should be done. In the early days in the Theatre it would have been impossible because of the religious use to which the building had originally been put. Later the strong non-conformist element among the leadership of the Society found the idea distasteful. By the nineteen sixties the chief remaining problem was that nearly £5,000 was still owing to the Rechabites, who had been generous and tolerant in keeping the rate of interest on the mortgage low and not pressing for repayment of the principal, but whose rules would not allow them to continue to help us if the premises became licensed. It was for this reason that Alan Gayton had worked so hard and so successfully to obtain the Corporation loan and to wind up our agreement with the Rechabites.

A further difficulty finding room for a bar which would hold all the members of a full audience who might want to use it. The solution was to use half of the Moyra Haywood Hall, the room which had been turned into a temporary theatre while the rebuilding took place after the fire. This had of course been in use, along with the Club-room, on the other side of the downstairs corridor, as a rehearsal room. But it was found that if it were partitioned off across the middle the remaining half still had enough floor space to accommodate a marked-out set almost the same size as the stage upstairs.

As to the half given over to the bar, I quote the announcement of its impending opening from the News Calendar of January/February 1966.

"THE NEW BAR

"We are pleased to announce that the new Theatre Bar will be opening on the 3rd February at 6p.m. From then on drinks will be available to Members and their guests and to patrons of shows from 6p.m. until 10.30p.m. every evening except Sunday. As well as beer, wines and spirits, coffee and snacks will also be served there instead of in the Canteen. We think you will be surprised by the change that has come over the rear end of the Moyra Haywood Hall. It's much larger than you'd imagine and the Bar Committee are to be congratulated on the good taste they have shown in the choice of decorations and fittings. It has a really comfortable theatre atmosphere without being gaudy or pretentious, and this has been achieved by the use of a scrumptious wall-to-wall carpet, modern wood panelling and subtle lighting. It'll be nice and warm too."

The capital needed to set up the bar was provided partly by the loan from the City Council and partly by a loan from the brewers (Bass, Mitchell and Butler) which was to be unrepayable so long as we continued to be their customers for ten years.

Another problem was the staffing of the bar, since it was felt that we had better not employ outside professional staff until it had become thoroughly established. The Society was much indebted to two members, Philip Berridge and Bill Ward, who together ran the bar in a most businesslike way for more than a year. Subsequently barmen have been employed. The bar did much to ease the Society's financial difficulties. Indeed, modern economic circumstances being what they are, it is hard to see how the Theatre could have continued to survive without the revenue accruing from it.

CHAPTER 8

From Sixties to Seventies

Some plays from the earlier half of this decade have already been mentioned. To these should be added the production by Neville Williams of *The Miracle Worker*, a powerful play by William Gibson about the remarkable education of Helen Keller. This was an early example of a talent which Neville has often displayed since, that of getting brilliant performances out of children, in this case Velma Holt. There was also a very sincere and moving performance by Nadine Jennings as Annie Sullivan.

The search for plays which would attract large audiences has sometimes been assisted by theatrical fashion, particularly by the nostalgia for the 'good old' Victorian and Edwardian days which has been such a feature of the anxious sixties and seventies. Music Hall is the most obvious example, and as well as improving the Society's bank balance this institution served to attract to the L.D.S. a number of members whose main talent was for singing and dancing and to give established members who possessed this talent the opportunity to display it. In the very first music hall, for instance, the leading singers were our own Jacqueline Shuttlewood; Mary Spencer, Betty Rice and Frank Billings, who had more often been seen, and heard, in productions by the musical societies; and José Johnson, with a foot, and a superb voice, in both camps. From this beginning a tradition has grown up. There has always been a high proportion of sketches, since we are primarily an acting society, and jugglers, acrobats and unicyclists are thin on the ground.

Another kind of production which proved popular for a while was the melodrama. Laurence Neal's staging of *Maria Marten* in 1964 was a great success. He used the version of Brian J. Burton, a Midland playwright. The author came to see it and was so pleased by the result that he offered us the chance to stage the première of his new adaptation of *Lady Audley's Secret*, which was duly presented in 1966, again under the direction of Laurence Neal. This production was shown to delegates to the Little Theatre Guild Conference who were our guests for the week-end. It was much enjoyed.

The vogue for melodrama declining, it was replaced some time later by one for Feydeau farces and for other farces of the same period.

As Alan Gayton and Geoffrey Burton gave up taking an active part in L.D.S. productions John Ghent began to establish himself as the Society's leading producer. He began in 1966 with a splendid production of Spewack's *My Three Angels* featuring a trio of fine, vigorous performances from Neville Williams, Robert Sansom and Roy Brown, the last of whom, after brilliantly playing Puck, again for John Ghent, in the following year, left us to pursue a successful professional career as Roy McCready.

In most of the succeeding seasons Ghent undertook two productions a year, maintaining a remarkably high standard, and it was he who produced the first of the Feydeaus, *Hotel Paradiso*, in 1970. When L.D.S. members are asked which is the funniest production they can remember this is the one which most of them name. This is what D.D. of the *Leicester Mercury* had to say about it:

"Timing is the essence of farce, and in the swiftly changing pattern of Georges Feydeau's situations in *Hotel Paradiso*, only the expert can hope to succeed.

"That is undoubtedly why producer John Ghent selected a 'first team' which included five Leicester Drama Society producers, and the irrepressible and experienced Ken Milton, to give impetus to the fast and furious fun at the Little Theatre, last night.

"Mr. Milton, also a producer in his own right, has been known to steal shows with a technique which combines the helpless desperation of Brian Rix and the slapstick resilience of Norman Wisdon. Last night, as the henpecked Monsieur Boniface, he faced formidable opposition. Formidable is the only word to describe Pauline Graham's towering performance as the dominating wife, losing not one opportunity to make it larger and even more colourful than life.

"Robert Martin was also an impressive challenger for best in show as the pompous architect, Monsieur Cot . . .

"Well in the running, too, were Margaret Mangan as his potentially unfaithful, but quickly disillusioned wife, and John Guillain, giving a Jon Pertwee quality to the stammering incoherence of Martin, the barrister . . .

"There was great merit, too, in the smaller parts . . . ."

One sort of modern play which the Society seems to do well and which is popular with our audiences is the historical play with a large cast, a genre which many of our leading playwrights seem to excel in. The main influence behind this kind of writing is that of Brecht, though he himself, apart from an extra end-of-term production of *Mother Courage*, has not up to now been represented in our programmes. But we have had Arthur Miller's *The Crucible* (1961), the play about the witches of Salem; Bolt's Sir Thomas More play, *A Man for all Seasons* (1963); *Luther* by John Osborne in 1965; *The Royal Hunt of the Sun* by Peter Shaffer in 1970; later, another Bolt play, *Vivat, Vivat Regina*, about Mary, Queen of Scots, and Elizabeth I in 1974; and, in 1976, Goldman's *A Lion in Winter*, which dealt with Henry II and his turbulent family.

These productions were all more or less successful, and several of them contained outstanding performances. Martin Caven gratefully and impeccably grasped the opportunity to represent the most sympathetic character in English history in Alan Gayton's production of *A Man for All Seasons*; and John Ghent, who had not yet turned to production, showed a thorough understanding of character and eloquent phrasing as Osborne's constipated theologian. The production was by Victor Bonfield, who was also responsible for *The Royal Hunt of the Sun*, one of the most popular plays of the last twenty years. He had a sturdy and credible Pizarro in Tony Ward, who also played two kings in this sequence of histories, Henries VIII and II; and Martin Caven gave another fine performance as the Inca Sun-King Atahuallpa. It was a closely debated decision to attempt this work, which some thought too ambitious for the size of our stage and our acting resources. But Kathie Layfield's well-designed permanent set and some good crowd work, as well as the performances I have mentioned, made it a success. It has often happened to the Society that plays which seemed as if they might be too difficult for us have proved to be most rewarding.

Two other productions of the late sixties which were particularly successful, and which owed their popularity not only to intrinsic merit, but also to the yearning for things past, were shows that came one after the other in 1968 – Laurence Neal's production of *Oh, What a Lovely War!* and Victor Bonfield's of Dodie Smith's *Dear Octopus*, a play which seemed to some of us too sentimental to merit revival, but of which our audience took a very different view.

The 1969 production of *Romeo and Juliet* marked the end of a remarkable sequence for Leslie Gillot. Since playing Voltimand in the 1927 *Hamlet* in which Roy Pochin was the Prince, he had appeared in all twenty-seven productions of plays by Shakespeare. He didn't play any of the big leading parts, though his roles included a number of noble dukes and a murderer or two; but leads were among the many parts he played – and is still playing at the time of writing – in other productions in what must be the Society's longest active career.

Since Geoffrey Burton gave up editing the News Calendar in the middle fifties this job had been done successively and ably by Leslie Walker, Douglas Goodlad, Martin Caven and David Millhouse. In 1967 it fell into the hands of Keith Miller, who had made some scathing comments at the A.G.M. about its conservative and uncritical attitudes. When invited to take it on himself, he renamed it *Focus*, gave it newspaper-style columns and roughly scrawled headlines, and through it set about the task of waking up the Society.

Keith Miller was perhaps the most atypical member the L.D.S. has ever had, though comparison might be made with Falconer Scott in the thirties. He hated any sort of dalliance with insignificant commercial plays, sought out grievances like a treasure-hunter with a metal detector, and hated compromise or polite insincerity. He had an astringent manner, not unlaced with humour. On committee he was no respecter of pronouncements from the chair and would not shut up. He made meetings longer and more acrimonious than ever before or since. But his *Focus* was certainly lively and may have done more good than harm; and he was an excellent producer of actors, though he usually gave them some eccentric gimmick to fight against, like the television camera that prowled about all over the set of *The Master Builder.* His best production was the very moving *A Scent of Flowers* (1970).

Speaking of committees, there was a major change for the Society in 1968. After ten years of very hard work and immense achievement, Geoffrey Burton and Alan Gayton, who had worked together so well as Chairman and Honorary Secretary, both decided that they must now give up. The work that they did on the rebuilding of the theatre and later on the new foyer literally changed the shape of the theatre and their influences on its artistic policies and standards were very great.

Burton wrote an article in *Focus* called "The Importance of Being Earnest", in which he spoke of his dream of being an impresario running his own theatre. It would be, he said, "a theatre with the highest artistic standards; the classics alternate with the avant-garde; the presentation is impeccable; talented young writers, actors and directors work in it."

Of the committee-run reality in Dover Street he wrote, "The beginnings of the Drama Society were rooted in a non-conformist tradition and its early members showed an earnestness which was reflected in their programmes; in their determination to establish their own theatre where they could put on plays which weren't available elsewhere in the city. To this earnestness was added the talents of others more artistically minded and together they made a formidable combination." For us, he said, "it may be that the way ahead lies in a greater austerity of choice. The finding of a new audience, perhaps, of a membership which is concerned with more than 'merely entertainment'. Since any organisation can only be a reflection of the total intellectual capacity of its membership, I am asking that we make ourselves better educated."

In the event it is the subsidised professional theatre which has become better educated, often getting in first – as is their right – with plays which we should have liked to do. For us the way ahead has lain, as usually, in compromise, not totally subservient to the Tyrant Box-Office, but not unaware of his looming presence; which is probably what Geoffrey, who is by no means an earnest person, really expected.

The new chairman was Orry Pochin, and the office of Honorary Secretary, the most arduous in the Little Theatre, was filled by Victor Bonfield.

CHAPTER 9

On to the Jubilees

When you have been going for a few decades and have two separate starting points, the jubilees begin to come thick and fast. After the Twenty-firsts and the Silvers we had to wait until 1971 for the 500th production in the Theatre; then the Goldens and the Diamonds, for the founding of the L.D.S. and the opening of the Little Theatre, were to follow. Some people like to forget their birthdays, but institutions like to remember them, feeling perhaps that survival is in itself an achievement. At all events, these occasions provide excuses for parties – and for fund-raising.

The 500th production took place in May 1971. It was *The Prime of Miss Jean Brodie*, produced by John Ghent, with Thea Craine in the lead giving a commanding performance. The three principal school-girls were played by Kathie Layfield, Jacqui Neal and Barbara Kenney, none of whom had really been a schoolgirl for quite a considerable time. That they were thoroughly convincing was a tribute to their youthful appearance and acting ability. It was a show worthy of the occasion.

A heartening feature at the beginning of the year had been the fact that two successive plays had brought unusually large audiences. The first of these was *Dracula*, produced by Pauline Graham, undertaken really as a bit of fun, with the success of the melodramas in mind. It caused a surprise by playing to almost full houses, which obviously included many people who did not usually attend the Theatre but who had succumbed to the same sort of attraction that makes horror films popular. Audiences of the same size, though presumably not of quite the same kind, also came to the next show, Bill Naughton's *Spring and Port Wine*, a north-country domestic comedy, which John Guillain produced. After this public support seemed generally to improve; so that in most seasons there have been one or two shows, besides the Christmas and Summer specials, which played to eighty or ninety per cent of capacity, while the play of average appeal has achieved something over sixty per cent and the most unpopular offerings have seldom dropped below fifty unless they have coincided with a blizzard or a heat-wave.

The greatest success of recent years, and the production which most people have named as the best they can remember, came in the 1972-3 season. This was *The Diary of Anne Franck*, another John Ghent production. The popularity of the second world war as a subject for film and drama had not yet reached its height, and some of us doubted whether this intensely moving, but harrowing, story of a Dutch Jewish family in hiding from the Nazis would be a draw. Others were convinced that it would, but I doubt if even the most optimistic ever dreamed that it would play to almost a hundred per cent. One of the reasons for its doing so must surely have been the excellence of the production. A loyal band of regular supporters will half-fill the theatre. Other factors determine how much of the remaining half is filled. One is the attraction of the title or the dramatist's name; a good press must be a help; and if there is something really outstanding the news gets round by word of mouth. All these factors must have been at work in this case.

Ken Milton, song and dance expert, debagged and misunderstood hero of so many farces, proved what some of us knew already: that he can be a sympathetic and powerfully moving actor in a straight emotional part. Thea Craine, so often his partner in light entertainment, brought a similar quality to the playing of his wife. For their daughter Anne John Ghent again used an experienced and mature actress, Stephanie Liggins, in the part of a child, with complete success; she looked right, sounded right and acted beautifully. There were fine performances too from Alice Spaul and Alastair Sutherland as the Van Damms and from Robert Sansom as Mr. Dussell.

All the programmes from 1972/3 bore the superscription 'Golden Jubilee Season' and the celebrations of this landmark culminated in the May Fair, the Jubilee Spring Fair at the County Rooms, an elegant setting eminently suitable for an artistic occasion, with the sole disadvantage that nobody could get their car anywhere near the building. It was well attended nevertheless, most notably by Sir Richard Attenborough, who had become our official Patron and who made a complimentary and encouraging speech. A prodigious work-load of knitting, bottling, pickling, cake-making, jamming, game-inventing, enbroidering, toy-stuffing, raffling; an assiduous collecting of old clothes, shoes, nearly-news, white elephants, books, plants and bottles; once more produced a satisfying profit, which was devoted to the great project of the seventies: the renovation of the auditorium, the only part of the building not refurbished since the fire.

Talking of dedicated work unrewarded by glory brings to mind backstage organisation again. The system was working well enough in general, but a decade during which fewer people seemed willing or able to devote all their leisure time to a single hobby brought its particular problems.

When Nigel Pochin had to give up the job of Senior Stage Manager he was succeeded by Stan Veasey, whose wife, Vera, was the very efficient head of the Wardrobe Department. Both of them found professional employment at the Haymarket Theatre, and Trevor Brook took over as S.S.M., continuing in the office for several years despite the fact that he was also the Society's Treasurer and therefore distinctly over worked. At the time of writing the job is shared by three people.

Backstage a handful of workers seemed to be present at every fit-up and every strike and whenever a close-season or emergency working party was called for. The Lighting department was lucky to have such figures of skill and authority as Geoffrey Sharp, Rob Thirlby and Charles Orr. But wardrobe and props became more and more of a chore and a worry as successive heads of these departments found it increasingly difficult to recruit competent helpers willing to take on the responsibility for shows and had to do more than their fair share themselves.

It was an excellent move when, in 1972, the Council decided to appoint Judy Nichol to run the hiring side of the wardrobe on a professional basis. So efficiently did she arrange and augment our stock and deal with the customers that the arrangement brought about both an improvement in the resources available for our own shows and a financial benefit to the Society. Recently the administration of the wardrobe department for the plays has also become a paid post.

But perhaps the most worrying single event of the seventies backstage was the retirement in 1974 of George Kelman. It had been realised a year or two before that George could not go on for ever, and there had been much, rather despairing, discussion about how he could possibly be replaced. Many, perhaps most, Little Theatres rely on amateur set designers and amateur scene painters. George had allowed us the best of both worlds. There was opportunity for members of the Society who were keen on designing: George would execute their designs, albeit somewhat reluctantly in some cases; but he could always be relied on for a design when required, and he carried out all the actual painting with a high degree of professional skill. With no tradition of amateur work in this field behind us, and with our heavy annual programme, it was agreed that a professional replacement would be necessary.

When the crisis finally came and the post was advertised it was found that there were skilful designers prepared to work in the amateur theatre for the sort of salary which the L.D.S. could afford, but in some respects we had to change our ways. Some of George's successors found if difficult to provide sets as far in advance of the production date as he had done; and, of course, they expected to design and not to be just carpenters and painters. They expected also to have a much greater say in matters of furniture and costume.

This followed a trend in the theatre at large, where the designer had for some years tended to become a much more important person. There had also been a trend away from the old box set with flats and towards a more permanent constructed set which called for skills of a rather different order.

David Kibart did some excellent work during the three years from

1975 to 1978 that he was at the Little; and early in 1979 John Hendrie, the designer at the time of writing, took over. He is a most versatile man of the theatre who takes a keen interest in properties and wardrobe, regarding them as an integral part of his design. If this diminishes to some extent the responsibility of members in these fields, it also solves a lot of problems and results in work of very high quality.

It was in 1974 that the big improvement to the auditorium took place. Until that year the floor of the theatre had only a slight slope, or rake, down towards the stage; so that the shorter members of the audience had always had to do a good deal of craning and peering between heads to follow the action on the stage. Many of the elderly seats had developed irregularities which made them austere, if not unstable, bases from which to watch an entertainment. It was decided that the auditorium should be given a much steeper rake – and that all the seats should be replaced. Lighting boards don't have such a long life as seats, and though a new one had been installed after the fire it was deemed to be no longer adequate. Another was urgently needed, and more space was needed in the lighting box.

First thoughts were that these things, together with the new curtains and carpets which would be necessary to complete the transformation, could not be afforded all at once; but the Committee and Council finally decided that if it could possibly be managed it would be more economical in the long run to carry out the whole programme, and that, with the help of a bank overdraft and an additional Corporation loan, the cost – of rather more than £25,000 – could be met. And so it proved.

The alterations, therefore, were extensive and impressive. The new rake rose neatly in shallow steps, and if it did not quite meet the requirement of providing a perfect view from every seat it certainly ensured that a lot more people could see without difficulty. A new forestage improved the feeling of contact between players and audience. The base of this was let into the floor at a lower level than the front of the auditorium, so that when the forestage was removed a partly sunken orchestra pit was created. The extended control room now stretched right across the back of the auditorium, providing adequate accommodation for sound as well as lighting technicians. You may remember that the 1930 seats were variously described as 'flame-coloured' and 'dull orange' and cost twenty-two shillings each. Those of 1974 were officially magenta, and cost as many pounds.

A lot of money was saved on this project by members doing themselves work which would otherwise have had to be paid for. This was particularly true in the lighting department. But the organiser and co-ordinator of the operation was the Honorary Secretary, Victor Bonfield.

With its completion we now had – if we had not before – what must have been one of the half-dozen best amateur-owned theatres in the country. Many of us who have been on Little Theatre Guild conferences have come back feeling very humble. We have seen theatres with the most discouraging difficulties; having to store scenery in a garage two streets away; having to rehearse in a cubby-hole; playing on a stage no bigger than our foyer, with entrances from one side only; making up in a dingy cellar, three or four to a mirror; seating an audience of ninety-two, some of them on wooden benches. And so often giving a brilliant performance.

We can, and should, be very proud of the Little Theatre, and think how lucky we are to have such a place to work in, and how much is owed to the founding fathers and the improvers along the way.

Fine facilities must be matched to fervour and talent and craftsmanship, and it takes a generous measure of these attributes to keep a programme of twelve shows a year going. The artistic record since the alterations shows the expected mixture of strengths and weaknesses.

It has to be admitted that actors and actresses of quality who are prepared to dedicate themselves to a play for a solid six weeks are not so easy to come by as they used to be. While it was thought necessary to put in an extra show in 1975 – Leslie Walker's production of *Ladies in Retirement* – to give a chance to some of the excellent actresses in the over-thirty-five group who were not getting as many parts as they deserved, there has been a marked shortage of leading men and of juveniles of both sexes. It is no longer easy to recruit the armies of spear-carriers and camp followers that could once be called into service. Committees during the last five years have felt, with great regret, that we could not assemble enough men able to speak verse adequately to do justice to a Shakespeare play, for so long an L.D.S.

My Three Angels (1966): Robert Sansom, Roy Brown and Neville Williams.

The Royal Hunt of the Sun (1970).

The Prime of Miss Jean Brodie (1971), the 500th production of the Leicester Drama Society.

Stephanie Liggins in *The Diary of Anne Franck* (1973).

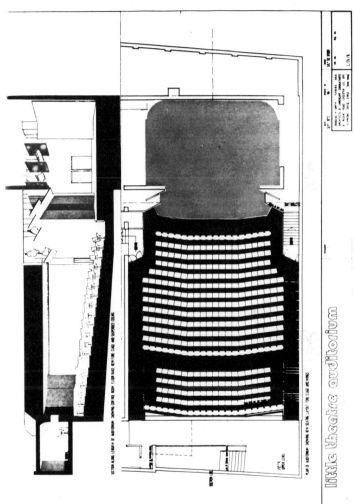

The architect's plan for the new auditorium, completed in 1974.

The Alchemist, produced at The Guildhall in 1955.

Dark of the Moon, the first play performed by the Society at the Minack Theatre, Porthcurno, Cornwall.

annual event. Currently the view is that we must somehow try again.

The demands of the box-office have also been a restricting factor, and the Society has felt bound to put on a number of rather ordinary plays, and a few rather bad ones, to cater for the taste for nostalgic revivals, farces and detective plays. So while the standard has remained generally high and there has been some excellent entertainment, it is hard to pick out high spots as obviously outstanding as in some former periods.

In 1975 Geoffrey Sharp, after years of trying, at last persuaded committee to let him stage the American *Detective Story* and scored a marked success with a play which has twenty-six characters. The next year, by way of contrast, there was a beautiful, but ill-attended production by Judith Pearson of Arbuzov's *The Promise* with a cast of three. This was delicately and sensitively played by Sue Astwood, Alan Mitchell and John Moore.

Crown Matrimonial, Ryton's play about the abdication of Edward VIII, which Barbara Kenney produced in 1977, was very popular and contained fine performances by Mary Angrave, who has done so much good work for the Society, as Queen Mary, Alan Mitchell as the King and John Ragg as Bertie.

The search for plays of quality by modern authors which would be acceptable to our audiences has been a chronic headache; and it was good to see, later in the same year, that Alan Bennett's *Habeas Corpus* was both commercially successful and greatly enjoyed. The vivacious production of this bizarre but hilarious play was by John Ghent. Another contemporary play which went well was *My Fat Friend* produced by John Saunders; but a serious modern American play, Anderson's *I Never Sang for my Father*, very well produced by Orry Pochin, though much enjoyed by those with a taste for serious drama, did not attract large audiences and provoked dissatisfied mutterings from people who did not care for a scene which showed some coffins.

The latter was in the 1978/9 season, during which there was also a very impressive production of Neville Williams of *The Innocents*, Archibald's dramatisation of *The Turn of the Screw*, notable for an excellent first set from John Hendrie and two more remarkable juvenile (ie: child) performances from Lucinda Edmonds and Richard Pearson.

But the popular successes of the season – artistic successes too – were two revue-type works not included in the plays for voucher-holders. John Ghent created and produced *A Talent to Amuse*, a comprehensive anthology of songs and sketches from the works of Noël Coward which could have played to full and enthusiastic audiences for three times as long as the one week it was allowed. And a spare week before Christmas was brilliantly filled by Thea Craine and Ken Milton with a revue called *All for Your Delight*, in the same vein as a number of after-show late-night entertainments they had previously given. They were admirably supported by their two pianists, Derrick Marshall and John Moore.

The ability to present entertaining and polished revue and cabaret work is perhaps to be expected from a good drama society, but it has been a particular strength of the L.D.S. in recent years, exemplified by those two 1978 shows, John Guillain's *Who's Pinched Me Tights?*, a pre-season extra in 1976, and very many Theatre Ball and party entertainments.

The manner of the Theatre's administration remained much as it had been for some time: the A.G.M. electing a General Committee, which then elected its own Production, Business and Promotions sub-committees, but now included three members of a Membership sub-committee elected directly from the A.G.M.; all under the benevolent eye of a Council which met once or twice a year and now mainly comprised long-serving active or once-active members of the Society. But there were a good many – in some cases disturbing – changes of personnel. The managership – with Michael Cocks retiring after fifteen years' service – the Chair and Secretaryship all changed hands more than once, like the post of stage designer. But by the time of the Golden Jubilee stability seemed to have been restored, with Victor Bonfield – an energetic and forceful secretary for ten years – now in the chair, Alan Mitchell in his place as secretary, and – to the general satisfaction of members – James O'Donoghue, for many years a popular acting member of the Society and its P.R.O., as manager.

CHAPTER 10

Extra-Mural Activities

Since 1930 almost all the productions of the Drama Society have naturally been staged at the Little Theatre, but there have been some notable exceptions.

The earliest of these was the *Pageant History of Henry the Eighth*, mentioned earlier. In November 1933 the Business Committee considered and approved the recommendation of the General Committee, "That at the request of the Council [ie: the Council of the L.D.S.], a Summer effort to reduce the Bank Loan by a substantial sum should be made, and that this effort should take the form of an open-air production of *Henry VIII* for a week under the direction of Mr. Frank Harwood . . .".

Mr. Harwood, a professional producer, agreed to produce the Pageant for a percentage of the takings (minimum: £50) and offered to produce some other of the Society's plays for nothing during the period of presentation. The Pageant was a major effort, and to mount it a special committee was set up, to be divided into six sub-committees. It took place in the De Montfort Hall Gardens (if wet, inside the De Montfort Hall) during the week June 18th-23rd 1934. The King was played by Rex Bradford Westwood and Wolsey by Roger Manvell, later to make a very high reputation as a film critic. Leslie Bowmar played Norfolk, and Roy Pochin Buckingham.

The Shakespeare play was given as a play within a play, as if it were performed to celebrate the bethrothal of James I's daughter, Elizabeth, to the Elector Palatine. Some idea of the scale of the undertaking is given by the following quotation from the Argument in the programme:

"Scene 12 . . . Making their bow before King James, the players make their exit. King James and his family depart for the Palace, and the remainder of the company, numbering two hundred, make their exit in the inspiring Helston Furry Dance."

Unfortunately all this splendour did nothing for the Bank Loan. The total expenditure was £504, the total receipts were £495; and the Executive Committee had to appeal for donations to cover the deficit.

During the war there were some forays by bands of individual members into outlying parts of the County, but not, I think, under the official aegis of the Society; and the next record I have of a performance outside the Theatre is of one in January 1952, when we were invited to take our production of *Don't Listen Ladies*, a charmingly stylish play, to the King's Lynn Arts Centre at the Guildhall of St. George at King's Lynn. It was a Sunday afternoon trip in a coach, with cast, back-stage helpers and Supporters' Club, and was much enjoyed. It was so well received that we were asked to make another contribution to the King's Lynn Festival in the following year. We took *Off the Record*, a naval farce, which seems to have proved too low-brow an entertainment to please the Festival organisers; and we were not asked again.

Another Guildhall was the scene of the next extramural activity, the fine fifteenth-century building in Leicester which often accommodated touring theatrical companies in Elizabethan and Jacobean times. In 1953 the City of Leicester Museum authorities had the brilliant idea of reviving the practice of performing plays there, and two years later the Drama Society was invited to present one. I was lucky enough to be the producer, and chose Ben Jonson's *The Alchemist*. Many of us had for a long time been wanting the Society to stage an Elizabethan or Jacobean play by an author other than Shakespeare, but it had always been decided that our audiences would not be so enthusiastic; so this was a welcome opportunity, and the setting of the Guildhall was marvellously appropriate.

The acting area was very small compared with the stage of the Theatre, but we were already used to being cramped, because this production took place in June 1955, just two months after the fire had driven us down to the little Little Theatre in the Moyra Haywood Hall, and we had found that physical limitations can be very stimulating. The stage was at the staircase end of the Guildhall, and we were able to use the balcony which runs across the end of the hall, and which is reminiscent of the gallery in the Shakespearean theatre, though there was hardly room for two people to squeeze past one another on it. There was no front curtain – and it was not so common at that time to manage without one as it is now – and only the simplest of permanent sets could be used.

Surprisingly, since *The Alchemist* is held by the literary to be one of the finest comedies in the language and had been done by the Old Vic Company a few years before, its bawdy proved too strong meat for one or two ladies who attended the first night, and a brisk rally of correspondence in the columns of the *Mercury* took pace, which may have helped to ensure that the end of the run played to better houses than the beginning.

The opening of *Everyman in his Humour*, the second of our Jonson plays at the Guildhall, produced by my wife, Pauline, in 1957, was also poorly attended. *The Guardian*, whose critic had been drawn to notice both shows by the eminence of the building, wrote, "There were several good performances which had the right sort of absorbed comic seriousness, and the general zest of the acting would have emerged better with more help from an audience whose insufficiency was equalled by its torpor". But this too picked up well as the run continued.

Certainly these shows were greatly enjoyed by those who took part, giving an extra satisfaction in addition to that usually associated with putting on a play: a feeling of privilege in being allowed to operate in such distinguished surroundings and to make an historical as well as a dramatic point.

The same kind of bonus is experienced when taking part in a production at the Minack Theatre, where the additional element is topographical rather than historical; and the shows we have taken to Cornwall form a sustained and extensive series of performances given outside the Theatre.

Interestingly enough the existence of this beautiful open-air theatre was brought to the notice of members of the Drama Society as long ago as 1933 in an article in the L.D.S. magazine by John Collard called "On the Cliffs Above Porthcurno". Lying on the sands of the lovely cove at Porthcurno the author asked someone about an advertisement he had seen for a performance of *Twelfth Night* and learnt "that each year one of Shakespeare's plays [was] performed in a little theatre built in the cliffs at the foot of the garden of the house of Cade". He could get there "by a little path leading up the cliff-face at the westward end of the cove".

"After much stumbling, slipping and losing of the way", he writes,

"Seats for four hundred people are set back in the cliff-face in tiers. Each row is turfed. A flight of steps leads down the centre, forming a gangway, from the gardens above, whence the public makes its entrance. To the left of this 'auditorium' there is a large rock, in front of which is a natural platform for chairs. I took this to be the Royal 'box' . . .

"The stage is as big as the Little Theatre's in area, and is built up and outwards from the sloping surface of the cliff. There is, of course, no roof or superstructure of any kind . . . Large rocks jutting out from the sides of the auditorium provide 'wings' and conceal dressing accommodation – they might have been placed there by Nature for this purpose . . ."

And on the performance: "The sound of the sea coming up from beyond the stage, sapphire blue deepening with the dusk and merging with the sky, and, perhaps, as Feste sings his last song, a crescent moon rising behind the rocks – a glorious tribute to the soul of Shakespeare".

The scene remains fundamentally the same. Many of the grassy seats have been replaced by concrete, and the stage, which still retained some grass when we first went to play there in 1964, is all concrete now. Other structures have been added, most of the labouring having been done by the redoubtable Miss Rowena Cade herself, with a single helper, at an age at which most people are sitting in comfortable arm-chairs with a rug over their knees. The need for some of the 'improvements' might be questioned, but the enchantment remains; and if the actors sometimes feel that they are being upstaged by the scenery, it more often enhances their work.

A number of people conspired together to start the Minack venture. There was, for instance, a native Cornishman in the person of Peter Gray, a lighting expert; but the prime mover was undoubtedly Geoffrey Sharp, who has produced many of the shows, and helped to administer, usually with Mary Angrave and Barbara Kenney, all of them.

Dark of the Moon was the play chosen for the first visit, and it proved to be an excellent choice. For one thing, it was a fairly daring one, since at this time the most frequently produced dramatist by a long way was still Shakespeare, and it was rare for a play outside the classical repertoire to be produced. For another, it was a play which required a large cast with many interesting small parts and a crowd – ideal for the many enthusiastic people keen to make the trip. Lastly, the outdoor scenes, especially the very atmospheric ones involving witches and conjure-people, could only gain from the setting.

The preparations were impressively thorough. Preliminary reconnaissance determined the exact size and shape of the stage – which, though similar in area to that of our own theatre as John Collard noted, is much wider and shallower – and revealed places where extra lamps could be put, and other opportunities for special effects, like the two tall pillars, on top of which the two witches could so bravely and effectively stand out with flowing draperies against the night sky. Many of the rehearsals were, by courtesy of Leicester University, who kindly lent us part of their grounds, held out of doors, so that the cast could get used to the extra projection needed for this kind of performance.

On the social side, accommodation was acquired in the school at Sennen – this was, alas, the last time that the entire team for a Minack production was quartered in one place – and two large barrels of beer were laid on, one for the school and one for the dressing room.

The event could hardly have been more successful. Regular customers at Minack found the play a refreshing change, as particularly suitable for outdoor performance as Geoffrey Sharp had been sure it would be, and the quality of the acting well above the average. The lighting was especially admired, for we had taken with us a lot of our own equipment to augment that which was provided, apparently an unusual procedure. We also took a lot of sound equipment and introduced innovations in this field. Its first function was to play by way of overture a spirited recording of "Don't Let the Rain Come Down", which became our signature tune at Minack.

Four years later, in an article in *The Times*, Miss Cade is quoted as saying that *Dark of the Moon* was one of the two productions at the Minack which she regarded as particularly outstanding – "so good you forgot you were watching a play at all".

We were invited to go again the next year, when we took Dryden's *Amphitryon*. The school was no longer available to us. We obtained the use of a smaller one, but some of us sybaritically preferred the superior comfort of 'The Old Success' at Sennen Cove; and in the ensuing years the company was dispersed in a variety of hotels, farmhouses, holiday flats, caravans and tents.

There have been no real failures at Minack, though some plays have obviously proved more suitable than others; and we have seldom lost more than one or two performances to bad weather.

We took plays to Cornwall for four successive years, but gradually many more dramatic societies got the same idea, and the demand for weeks at Minack became so great that we had to wait two years, and finally three years, for a turn.

Everyone who has declaimed, or manned a spotlight, or sewn on buttons or sold jellied eels under a summer evening sky in that cliffside amphitheatre has some happy memories. The one that springs first to my mind is of the night the lights failed.

It was during the revival meeting scene in *Inherit the Wind*. The congregation was assembled and the service had begun when suddenly we were plunged, through absolutely no fault of our electricians, into darkness. But the show went on. Within a few seconds contingency plans had been put into effect, and kneeling figures punctuated the arc formed by the front edge of the stage shining big torches at the faces of those with lines to say.

The scene contains the words, "God said, 'Let there be light, and there was light'". Memories are inexact, and it is tempting to think that it was at this point that the power was restored. I don't really believe it was so, but certainly those lines became comedy lines and it was not long after that the lights came back again and the crisis was over.

The complete list of plays performed at Minack, with their producers, is as follows:

1964	Dark of the Moon	Geoffrey Sharp
1965	Amphytrion	Geoffrey Sharp
1966	Toad of Toad Hall	John Northam
1967	The Hostage	Laurence Neal
1969	The Recruiting Officer	Geoffrey Sharp
1970	Music Hall	Geoffrey Sharp
1972	Inherit the Wind	Geoffrey Sharp
1974	The Skin of Our Teeth	John Graham
1976	The Yellow Jacket	José Cooke & Barbara Kenney
1979	Treasure Island	John Saunders

There have, of course, been many minor excursions beyond the walls of the Theatre in response to requests for cabaret-type entertainments or poetry readings or talks on various theatrical topics. On a much bigger scale has been the series of Music Halls which Jacqueline Shuttlewood has organised, not necessarily using material from the main annual Music Hall, and taken to many stages, large and small, all over the county. These seem to have been greatly enjoyed and have provided welcome extra revenue for the Theatre.

CHAPTER 11

Some Conclusions

I can't forbear to add a sort of whence-and-whither section to what I feel even a more objective observer would see as a story of very considerable achievement.

For many years the Society's programmes carried the following statement:

'The Little Theatre is owned by the Leicester Drama Society, whose aim is to present plays of good quality to the General Public. The Society was formed to promote the study and practice of Drama by means of discussions, play readings, instructional courses and a library.'

This is not too clearly expressed. There doesn't seem a sufficient connection between the two sentences. But I suppose we all know what it meant.

The programmes now tell us:

'The Little Theatre is owned by the Leicester Drama Society, a non-profit making organisation founded in 1922 for the furtherance and study of the art of drama. It presents a repertoire of plays of all types through the year, and, with its club-rooms, bar and library forms a social meeting place for those interested in the theatre.'

The changes suggest a tactical withdrawal from the position previously held with regard to the quality of the plays, and a change of emphasis, despite the retention of the word "study", from the didactic to the social. This is in keeping with the mood of the times – the importance of not being earnest.

So to what extent have the aims of the founders been carried out, to what extent missed, and to what extent deliberately modified? Let us consider the one about the presentation of plays of good quality. Whether you think this has been achieved or not depends very much on how you define the term. But since the number of plays produced now exceeds six hundred, and the sternest critic could hardly deny that a high proportion of them have been good ones, it can safely be asserted that a great many plays of good quality have been presented.

If we take the aim to have been to present plays of good quality *and no other*, then we are on less sure ground. I think I may have let slip a hint or two that I think some of the plays which have been produced could only be so described by the sort of person who prefers Golden Delicious to Cox's Orange Pippin. That a few undeserving specimens should have been allowed to slip through the sieve of critical discernment is only natural; and that some have been allowed deliberately and cynically to by-pass it can be excused on the grounds of economic necessity; so long as it remains only a few and the matter is subject to constant vigilance.

The aims did not state that we should present *all sorts* of plays of good quality. This has never been possible. The present difficulty with regard to the classics has already been referred to; so have the problems regarding the production of many contemporary plays which arise from the fact that we present plays to the General Public and not to a select coterie of students of Drama. The dilemma posed by the new school of writing which followed Osborne's lead in 1956 has become more acute.

Ayckbourn is the only modern dramatist of quality who is generally popular. Two plays by Peter Nicholls have proved acceptable, as has much of the work of Robert Bolt and Peter Shaffer, though it should be noted that as things stand at present it would be considered rashly daring to stage *Equus* because of the nude scene.

The fact remains that the list of authors who are highly regarded by drama critics and whose work has not been seen in the main programme at the Little is a very long one. It includes Howard Barker, Edward Bond (though there was an admirable two-night production of *The Bundle* by the Arena group), Howard Brenton, Simon Gray, Trevor Griffiths, Christopher Hampton, David Hare, Stephen Poliakov, Tom Stoppard, David Storey, Edward Whitehead and Charles Wood.

The extent of this list suggests several possibilities: (a) that the critics are wrong; (b) that the L.D.S. is too cautious in its consideration of the work of contemporary dramatists and too apprehensive of possible box-office failure; (c) that talented modern writers have lost touch with the General Public, like some of their colleagues in the spheres of art and music, and are writing for an élitist minority.

Certainly I can sympathise with some of the feelings which we ascribe, rightly or wrongly, to our audiences: that some dramatists take too dark a view of the world today and therefore present a distorted picture of it by portraying too many unsympathetic characters and too many acts of gratuitous violence, by seeming obsessed with the more unorthodox aspects of sex and by using "bad" language simply for the pleasure of shocking rather than for any dramatic force it may have.

On the other hand this would be a very unfair assessment of the work of many of the writers on the list. Some unpleasantness may have to be faced in the interest of producing a serious and sincere play, or indeed a very funny one. Tom Stoppard, perhaps the most brilliant writer on the list, is thought inaccessible because of the too considerable intellectual content of his work. A great pity.

It brings me anyway to the matter of promoting 'the study and practice of drama'. It might be said that the L.D.S. is so busy with the practice that it has no time for the study, that if for one reason or another we can't perform the classics and many of the moderns at least we ought to know about them, to be reading and discussing them. If in the Geoffrey Burton manner, I were postulating a Utopian drama society, it would find time and room for classes or study groups in the history of Drama and in various theoretical and practical aspects of the subject; and it would include a studio where members interested in minority theatre could act or at least read plays which come into this category without bothering the General Public with them.

But no criticism is intended. Countless attempts have been made during the last sixty years. Play reading groups have been organised and have dissolved. Successive membership committees have arranged talks on drama and discussions and performances, which have usually been ill-attended and so discouraged further efforts. Still, there are possibilities to be borne in mind for some future reorganisations.

At one time we did enthusiastically discuss our own productions. Particularly in the fifties Crit. Nights – evening members' meetings at which the previous week's production was discussed, with the producer there to defend himself and his cast – were popular and drew large audiences. But some producers didn't like them, some members felt that they became too self-congratulatory on the one hand or too acrimonious on the other, and their popularity dwindled. Eventually only the cast and a few old faithfuls came to listen. The practice has never been altogether abandoned, but it has become intermittent and without interest for the majority of members.

If the inability to persuade members to take an interest in discussing drama has been one of the Society's failures, there have been many compensating successes on the membership side. There have been a lot of excellent social events – regular Theatre Balls and Christmas Parties, and other celebrations like Hallowe'en Parties and Gala Nights.

For many years there have been classes for young people and others who wished to practise the craft of acting. These have been variously called The Student Group, Actors' Studio and, at present, Arena; and they have met every Thursday night during the season under the enthusiastic guidance of a series of dedicated organisers like John Ghent, Brenda Milton, Joanne Runswick, José Johnson and Kathie Layfield. They have all stimulated great interest and a lot of hard work, and if the gap between the group and the stage upstairs has proved hard to bridge in all but a few cases the fault has not been theirs. A more recent addition to this coaching programme has been the regular Saturday morning sessions for school children, still too young to be full members of the Society, to which Christine Hewson and her helpers are applying themselves so energetically.

But, of course, the plays are the main thing. Most people join the L.D.S. because they are interested in acting in, producing, or helping in the production of plays; and it is by the quality of the plays that the Society has been and will be judged. That audiences have been more often than not satisfied has been proved by their continued support. If I had suggested that the Society and the Theatre were deserving only of unqualified praise I should have been rightly disbelieved. If I did not admit to the great pride I feel in the organisation of which I have written, I should be reticent to the point of dishonesty. And I am conscious of not having adequately expressed the immense pleasure and satisfaction which membership of the L.D.S. has given to the hundreds of us whose privilege it has been to contribute to the work the Society has done during these sixty not inglorious years.

Productions of Leicester Drama Society 1922-80

Title	Author	Producer
	1922	
The Silver Box	Galsworthy	Frank Clewlow
Triple Bill:		
X = 0	John Drinkwater	Frank Clewlow
The Cobbler's Shop	Charles Forrest	
The Workhouse Ward	Lady Gregory	
The Fantasticks	Edmond Rostand	Frank Clewlow
Candida	Shaw	R. F. Rattray
	1923	
Strife	Galsworthy	Frank Clewlow
The Cassilis		
Engagement	E. C. St. J. Hankin	Frank Clewlow
Othello	Shakespeare	Frank Clewlow
	1924	
An Enemy of the People	Ibsen	Frank Clewlow
The Merry Wives of		
Windsor	Shakespeare	Frank Clewlow
	1925	
Outward Bound	Sutton Vane	Geoffrey Mead
The Ship	St. John Ervine	Geoffrey Mead
	1926	
The Romantic Young		
Lady	G. Martinez Sierra	Horace Twilley
Romeo and Juliet	Shakespeare	Geoffrey Mead
Autumn Fire	T. G. Murray	Geoffrey Mead

1927/28

Hamlet	Shakespeare	Frank Toone/
		H. Pochin
Ambrose Applejohn's		
Adventure	Hackett	Harry Letts
The Highway	Eric Pochin	Geoffrey Mead
The Dover Road	A. A. Milne	Harry Letts
{ *His Lordship's Wooing*	H. G. Sharman*	H. Twilley
The Door	Moyra Haywood*	Geoffrey Mead
A Jazz Processional	Mary Waddington*	Eric Pochin

*Winning plays in one-act play competition

1928/29

A Bit o'Love	Galsworthy	William Langley
Twelfth Night	Shakespeare	Geoffrey Mead
The Cradle Song	G. Martinez Sierra	Harry Letts

1929/30

A Florentine Tragedy	Oscar Wilde	Geoffrey Mead
Hassan	James Elroy Flecker	Harry Letts
The Circle	W. Somerset	
	Maugham	Geoffrey Mead
The Skin Game	Galsworthy	*
The Knight of the		
Burning Pestle	Sir Francis Beaumont	*
Outward Bound	Sutton Vane	Geoffrey Mead

*No producer credited in programme

1930/31

Loyalties	John Galsworthy	Geoffrey Mead
Mary Rose	J. M. Barrie	Harry Letts
The Silver Chord	Sidney Howard	Moyra Haywood
The Devil's Disciple	Shaw	Geoffrey Mead
The Shoemaker's Holiday	Thomas Dekker	H. Pochin
A Hundred Years Old	The Brothers Quintero	Doreen O'Driscoll
The Importance of		
Being Earnest	Oscar Wilde	A. H. Davy

The Soul of Nicholas		
Snyders	J. K. Jerome	William Langley
The Rising Sun	Herman Heijermans	Geoffrey Mead
Captain Brassbound's		
Conversion	Shaw	Herbert Pochin

1931/32

St. Joan	Shaw	Geoffrey Mead
The Cradle Song	G. Martinez Sierra	Bert Sutton
French Leave	Reginald Berkeley	Leslie Bowmar
What the Public Wants	Arnold Bennett	Walter Martin
Charles and Mary	Joan Temple	Doreen O'Driscoll
The Pigeon	Galsworthy	Herbert Pochin
By Candlelight	Harry Graham	Geoffrey Mead
Doctor Knock	Jules Romains	Roy Pochin
A Murder has been		
Arranged	Emlyn Williams	Geoffrey Mead
A Bill of Divorcement	Clemence Dane	Moyra Haywood
And So To Bed	J. B. Fagan	Westboro' Martin
The Ship	St. John Ervine	W. K. Bedingfield
The Merry Wives of		
Windsor	Shakespeare	Geoffrey Mead

1932/33

The Lady with the Lamp	Reginald Berkeley	Herbert Pochin
Mr. Faintheart	Ian Hay	Moyra Haywood
The Rose without a Thorn	Clifford Bax	Geoffrey Mead
The Land of Promise	W. Somerset	
	Maugham	William Langley
The Second Mrs.		
Tanqueray	A. W. Pinero	Walter Martin
The Tyrant	Rafael Sabatini	Roy Pochin
The Rivals	R. B. Sheridan	J. K. Peel
The Liars	Henry Arthur Jones	Walter Martin
She Passed Through		
Lorraine	Lionel Hale	H. Pochin
Pygmalion	Shaw	Geoffrey Mead
Down our Street	Ernest George	Moyra Haywood

Quality Street	J. M. Barrie	Harry Letts
The Merchant of Venice	Shakespeare	Geoffrey Mead

1933/34

Martine	Jean-Jacques Bernard	H. Pochin
The Show	Galsworthy	Geoffrey Mead
You Never Can Tell	Shaw	J. K. Peel
The Breadwinner	W. Somerset Maugham	Leslie Bowmar
Journey's End	R. C. Sherriff	Frank Harwood
The Eternal Spring	Peter Garland	Doreen O'Driscoll
R.U.R.	Karel Čapek	Moyra Haywood
Island Treasure	R. Eric Pochin	R. Eric Pochin
Outward Bound	Sutton Vane	Geoffrey Mead
Dear Brutus	J. M. Barrie	Walter Martin
Arms and the Man	Shaw	Frank Harwood
A Bit o'Love	Galsworthy	William Langley
Sheppey	W. Somerset Maugham	Frank Harwood
Children in Uniform	Christa Winsloe	Frank Harwood
Much Ado about Nothing	Shakespeare	Geoffrey Mead
Yellow Leaves	Ethel Boileau	Frank Harwood

1934/35

The Man with a Load of Mischief	Ashley Dukes	Herbert Pochin
The Would-be Gentleman	Molière	Leslie Bowmar
Hobson's Choice	Harold Brighouse	H. L. Midgley
The Truth About Blayds	A. A. Milne	J. Rylett-Salew
Nine Day's Wonder	Geoffrey Mead	J. Rylett-Salew
Candida	Shaw	Roger Manvell
Christopher Columbus	Eric Pochin	J. Rylett-Salew
On Approval	Frederick Lonsdale	Geoffrey Mead
The Rising Generation	Wyn Weaver & Laura Leycester	J. Rylett-Salew
Another Language	Rose Franken	J. Rylett-Salew
Is Life Worth Living?	Lennox Berkeley	J. Rylett-Salew
Eight Bells	Percy G. Maudley	Harry Letts

If Four Walls Told	Edward Percy	Roy Pochin
Mariners	Clemence Dane	Geoffrey Mead
The Kingdom of God	G. Martinez Sierra	J. Rylett-Salew
Getting Married	Shaw	J. Rylett-Salew
Macbeth	Shakespeare	Geoffrey Mead
The Importance of		
Being Ernest	Oscar Wilde	J. Rylett-Salew
Juno and the Paycock	Sean O'Casey	J. Rylett-Salew

1935/36

Old English	Galsworthy	William Langley
Abraham Lincoln	John Drinkwater	Geoffrey Mead
Lady Precious Stream	S. I. Hsuing	Doreen O'Driscoll
The Apple Cart	Shaw	Herbert Pochin
The Whiteheaded Boy	Lennox Robinson	Moyra Haywood
Major Barbara	Shaw	H. Lee Midgley
Toad of Toad Hall	A. A. Milne	Geoffrey Mead
Escape	Galsworthy	Moyra Haywood
Potash and Perlmutter	Montague Glass	Walter Martin
Charles Rex	Geoffrey Mead	Geoffrey Mead
Colonel Wotherspoon	James Bridie	Moyra Haywood
Inheritors	Susan Glaspell	Roy Pochin
The Way of the World	William Congreve	Frank Harwood
Henry IV – Part I	Shakespeare	Geoffrey Mead

1936/37

Queen of Scots	Gordon Daviot	Roy Pochin
Noah	André Obey	Geoffrey Mead
Yellow Sands	Eden & Adelaide	
	Philpotts	H. Lee Midgley
Bees on the Boatdeck	J. B. Priestley	Moyra Haywood
Androcles and the Lion/		
The Shewing up of		Herbert Pochin/
Blanco Posnet	Shaw	Albert Northfold
The Cherry Orchard	Anton Chekov	Doreen O'Driscoll/
		Marian Pickard
Hanky Panky	Bert Voss	Geoffrey Mead

The Moon in the Yellow River	Denis Johnstone	Moyra Haywood
{ *Too True to be Good*	Shaw	Albert Northfold
{ *The Two Shepherds*	G. Martinez Sierra	Geoffrey Mead
The Betrayal	Padraic Colum	Doreen O'Driscoll
Semper Eadem	Eric Pochin	Eric Pochin
The School for Scandal	R. B. Sheridan	Frank Harwood
Hay Fever	Noël Coward	Moyra Haywood
Julius Caesar	Shakespeare	Geoffrey Mead

1937/38

The Composite Man	Ronald Jeans	Moyra Haywood
Antony and Anna	St. John Ervine	Frank Harwood
St. Helena	R. C. Sherriff/	
	Jeanne de Casilis	Geoffrey Mead
The Black Eye	James Bridie	Doreen O'Driscoll
The Old Ladies	Rodney Ackland	Marian Pickard/
		Moyra Haywood
Spring Tide	George Billam	Roy Pochin
Alice in Wonderland	Lewis Carroll/	
	R. Eric Pochin	R. Eric Pochin
Parnell	Elsie T. Schauffler	Geoffrey Mead
After October	Rodney Ackland	Maurice Westhead
Pride and Prejudice	Helen Jerome	Frank Harwood
A Month in the Country	Ivan S. Turgenev	Marian Pickard/
		Moyra Haywood
The Millionairess	Shaw	A. Northfold
Down Our Street	Ernest George	Moyra Haywood
Othello	Shakespeare	Geoffrey Mead

1938/39

In Theatre Street	H. R. Lenormand	Moyra Haywood/
		Marian Pickard
Boyd's Shop	St. John Ervine	Moyra Haywood
Remember Sparta	Geoffrey Mead	Geoffrey Mead
The Road to Rome	Robert E. Sherwood	Moyra Haywood
Dangerous Corner	J. B. Priestley	Maurice Westhead

Through the Looking Glass	Lewis Carroll/ Eric Pochin	R. Eric Pochin
The Brontës	Alfred Sangster	Moyra Haywood
Climbing	Marten Cumberland	Albert Northfold
On the Rocks	Shaw	Moyra Haywood
The Taming of the Shrew	Shakespeare	Geoffrey Mead
A Doll's House	Ibsen	Marian Pickard/ Moyra Haywood
The Anatomist	James Bridie	R. Eric Haywood
Hamlet	Shakespeare	Geoffrey Mead
Whiteoaks	Mazo de la Roche	Maurice Westhead
The Doctor's Dilemma	Shaw	Moyra Haywood

1939/40

Jane Eyre	Helen Jerome	Moyra Haywood
I Have Been Here Before	J. B. Priestley	Moyra Haywood
The Farmer's Wife	Eden Philpotts	Geoffrey Mead
Hay Fever	Noël Coward	Moyra Haywood

1940/41

Laburnum Grove	J. B. Priestley	Moyra Haywood
What Happened to George	G. F. Bradby/ Vera Beringer	Moyra Haywood
Bird in Hand	John Drinkwater	Moyra Haywood
Escape	Galsworthy	Moyra Haywood
Robert's Wife	St. John Ervine	Moyra Haywood
Promise	Henry Bernstein	Moyra Haywood

1941/42

Alice, Thomas and Jane	Enid Bagnold/ Vera Beringer	Moyra Haywood
Badger's Green	R. C. Sherriff	Moyra Haywood
Thunder Rock	Robert Ardrey	Moyra Haywood
Time and the Conways	J. B. Priestley	Moyra Haywood

1942/43

Glorious Morning	Norman Macowan	Moyra Haywood

What Happened to George	G. F. Bradby/ Vera Beringer	Moyra Haywood
Treasure Island	J. B. Fagan	Moyra Haywood/ Harry Martin
Take Two from One	G. Martinez Sierra	Marian Pickard
The Little Minister	James Barrie	Walter Martin
Dear Octopus	Dodie Smith	Marian Pickard

1943/44

The Late Christopher Bean	Emlyn Williams	Marian Pickard
Toad of Toad Hall	A. A. Milne	Harry Martin
He Who Gets Slapped	Leonid N. Andreyev	A. E. Christopherson
An Ideal Husband	Oscar Wilde	Marian Pickard
You Can't Take it With You	Moss Hart & George Kaufmann	Harry Martin
A Midsummer Night's Dream	Shakespeare	John Bourne

1944/45

People at Sea	J. B. Priestley	Marian Pickard
I'll Leave it to You	Noël Coward	Walter Martin
Tobias and the Angel	James Bridie	Harry Martin
The Rose and the Ring	Harris Deans	John Bourne
Magic	G. K. Chesterton	Lindley Richardson
The Crown of St. Felice	F. Sladen Smith	A. E. Christopherson
Blithe Spirit	Noël Coward	Harry Martin
Fanny's First Play	Shaw	Emmie Bent
They Came to a City	J. B. Priestley	Albert Northfold/ Roy Pochin
In Good King Charles' Golden Days	Shaw	A. E. Christopherson
Yellow Sands	Eden Philpotts	Lindley Richardson

1945/46

Claudia	Rose Franken	Emmie Bent

Drum on the Shore	Leslie Walker	Leslie Walker/ Harry Martin
Friends and Relations	St. John Ervine	A. Northfold
Alice in Wonderland	Lewis Carroll/ Eric Pochin	Lindley Richardson
Mr. Bolfry	James Bridie	Harry Martin
The Corn is Green	Emlyn Williams	Leonard Bridges
Mr. Pim Passes By	A. A. Milne	Harry Martin
St. Joan	Shaw	A. E. Christopherson
Victoria Regina	Laurence Housman	Albert Northfold
Ladies in Retirement	Edward Percy/ Reginald Denham	Edward Lord

1946/47

The Barretts of Wimpole Street	Rudolf Besier	Anthony Harris
The Important of Being Earnest	Oscar Wilde	Leslie Bowmar
Shadow and Substance	Paul Vincent Carrol	Emmie Bent
Treasure Island	J. B. Fagan	Harry Martin
Dust Among the Stars	Geoffrey Mead	Geoffrey Mead
The Flashing Stream	Charles Morgan	Eric Pochin
Uncle Vanya	Chekhov	Emmie Bent
Crisis in Heaven	Eric Linklater	A. E. Christopherson
Twelfth Night	Shakespeare	Geoffrey Mead

1947/48

Love from a Stranger	Frank Vosper	Robert Martin
Berkley Square	John L. Balderstone/ J. C. Squire	Kathleen Christopherson/ Pauline Smart
Mrs. Warren's Profession	Shaw	Emmie Bent
The Light of Heart	Emlyn Williams	Geoffrey Mead
Richard of Bordeaux	Gordon Daviot	A. E. Christopherson
The Glass Slipper	Eleanor & Herbert Farjeon	Leslie Walker
The Little Foxes	Lillian Hellman	Laurence Neal

Mungo's Mansion	Walter Macken	Anthony Harris
Dark Victory	George Brewer/	
	Bertram Bloch	Eric Pochin
The Winter's Tale	Shakespeare	Albert Northfold
The Shining Hour	Keith Winter	Geoffrey Burton
The Circle	W. Somerset	
	Maugham	Roy Pochin
The Middle Watch	Ian Hay/	
	Stephen King-Hall	Gilbert Gillard

1948/49

The Wind of Heaven	Emlyn Williams	Emmie Bent
Vanity Fair	W. M. Thackeray/	
	Constance Cox	Geoffrey Mead
Of Mice and Men	John Steinbeck	A. E. Christopherson
The Winslow Boy	Terence Rattigan	Geoffrey Burton
Little People of the River	Eric Pochin	Eric Pochin
Hedda Gabler	Henrik Ibsen	Geoffrey Burton
The Guardsman	Forenc Molnár	A. E. Christopherson
The Voysey Inheritance	Harley Granville	
	Barker	Arthur Morris
Richard III	Shakespeare	Frank Harwood
When We Are Married	J. B. Priestley	Albert Northfold
The Witch	John Masefield	Kathleen
		Christopherson/
		Pauline Smart
Little by Little	Geoffrey Burton	
	& others	Geoffrey Burton

1949/50

An Inspector Calls	J. B. Priestley	Arthur Morris
The Playboy of the		
Western World	J. M. Synge	Eric Pochin
Portrait of a Queen	Geoffrey Mead	Geoffrey Mead
Love in Idleness	Terence Rattigan	Emmie Bent/
		David Lyall
Toad of Toad Hall	A. A. Milne	Geoffrey Burton

Village Wooing	Shaw	Albert Northfold
The Man of Destiny		
The Poltergeist	Frank Harvey	Alan Gayton
A Man's House	John Drinkwater	Anthony Harris
The Giaconda Smile	Aldous Huxley	David Lyall
Caste	T. W. Robertson	Gilbert Gillard
Tonight at 8.30	Noël Coward	Victor Bonfield/
		Pauline Smart/
		Laurence Neal

1950/51

Playbill	Terence Rattigan	Leslie Walker
Our Town	Thornton Wilder	Geoffrey Burton
The Servant of Two		
Masters	Carlo Goldoni	Roy Pochin
Miss Mabel	R. C. Sherriff	Alan Gayton
Sinbad the Sailor	Geoffrey Burton/	
	Eric Pochin	Geoffrey Burton
The Man with a Load of		
Mischief	Ashley Dukes	Anthony Harris
Bonaventure	Charlotte Hastings	Eric Pochin
Little Lambs Eat Ivy	Noel Langley	Albert Northfold
King Lear	Shakespeare	Goeffrey Mead
The Indifferent Shepherd	Peter Ustinov	Alan Gayton
The Apple Cart	Shaw	A. E. Christopherson
Youth at the Helm	P. Vulpius	
	(trans. H. Griffith)	Victor Bonfield

1951/52

Captain Carvallo	Denis Cannan	David Lyall
Winterset	Maxwell Anderson	Robert Martin
The Clandestine Marriage	George Colman/	
	David Garrick	Geoffrey Burton
Don't Listen, Ladies	Sacha Guitry	Alan Gayton
Beauty and the Beast	Nicholas S. Gray	Eric Pochin/
		Albert Northfield
The Wild Duck	Ibsen	Emmie Bent

They Got What They Wanted	Louis D'Alton	David Lyall
Venus Observed	Christopher Fry	Geoffrey Burton
Caesar's Friend	Campbell Dixon/	
	Dermot Morrah	Leslie Walker
The Merchant of Yonkers	Thornton Wilder	Pauline Graham
The Merry Wives of Windsor	Shakespeare	Geoffrey Mead
Off the Record	Ian Hay/	
	Stephen King-Hall	Gilbert Gillard

1952/53

The Rivals	R. B. Sheridan	Geoffrey Burton
The Glass Menagerie	Tennessee Williams	Alan Gayton
Romeo and Juliet	Shakespeare	Anthony Harris
Black Chiffon	Lesley Storm	Laurence Neal
Alice in Wonderland	Lewis Carroll/	
	Eric Pochin	John Graham
The Late Edwina Black	William Dinner &	
	William Morum	Leslie Walker
Diary of a Scoundrel	Rodney Ackland	Victor Bonfield
The Lady's Not For Burning	Christopher Fry	Alan Gayton
Hobson's Choice	Harold Brighouse	David Lyall
The Admirable Crichton	J. M. Barrie	Paul Wightman
Man and Superman	Shaw	Leslie Walker
On Monday Next	Philip King	David Lyall

1953/54

The Miser	Molière/Malleson	John Thacker
Return to Tyassi	Benn Levy	Alan Gayton
Othello	Shakespeare	Geoffrey Burton
The Male Animal	Jas. Thurber &	
	Elliott Nugent	John Graham
What Happened to George?	Vera Beringer	Wendy Wright
The Three Sisters	Chekhov	Geoffrey Burton
Ring Round the Moon	Jean Anouilh	Alan Gayton

The River Line	Charles Morgan	Laurence Neal
Dandy Dick	A. W. Pinero	Gilbert Gillard
Juno and the Paycock	Sean O'Casey	John Thacker
Home at Seven	R. C. Sherriff	Victor Bonfield
The Yellow Jacket	George C. Hazelton/	
	Benrimo	Pauline Graham

1954/55

Waters of the Moon	N. C. Hunter	Wendy Wright
Pygmalion	Shaw	Alan Gayton
The Sleeping Clergyman	James Bridie	Geoffrey Burton
The Happy Marriage	John Clements	Eric Cheeney
Treasure Island	Stevenson/Fagan	Stawley
The Deep Blue Sea	Terence Rattigan	Laurence Neal
Noah	André Obey	Geoffrey Burton
The Merchant of Venice	Shakespeare	John Thacker
The Love of Four Colonels	Peter Ustinov	Robert Martin/
		Alan Gayton
To Live in Peace	Victor Rietti	Pauline Graham
Private Lives	Noël Coward	John Chambers
Nightmare Abbey	T. L. Peacock	John Thacker
The Alchemist	Ben Johnson	John Graham
(at the Guildhall)		

1955/56

The Doctor's Dilemma	Shaw	Eric Cheeney
The Castiglione Bros.	Alberto Colantuoni	Leslie Walker
Crime Passionel	Jean-Paul Sartre	John Graham
The Confidential Clerk	T. S. Eliot	Alan Gayton
Tobias and the Angel	James Bridie	David Lyall
Doctor's Joy	Molière/Charles Drew	Laurence Neal
A Question of Fact	Wynyard Brown	Derek Burrows
Pillars of the Community	Ibsen	Pauline Graham
The Whiteheaded Boy	Lennox Robinson	Paul Wightman
The Prisoner	Bridget Boland	Wendy Wright
Anastasia	Marcelle-Maurette	David Lyall
Antigone/A Phoenix too		
Frequent	Jean Anouilh/	
	Christopher Fry	John Graham

1956/57

The Burning Glass	Charles Morgan	Victor Bonfield
Candida	Shaw	Derek Burrows
The Living Room	Graham Greene	Alan Gayton
Present Laughter	Noël Coward	David Lyall
Harvey	Mary Chase	Emmie Bent
Dragon's Mouth	Jacquetta Hawkes/	
	J. B. Priestley	Douglas Goodlad
The Sleeping Prince	Terence Rattigan	Geoffrey Burton
Ghosts	Ibsen	John Graham
Waiting for Gillian	Ronald Millar	John Chambers
All My Sons	Arthur Miller	Wendy Wright
A Kind of Folly	Owen Holder	Alan Gayton/
		Gilbert Gillard
Dr. Angelus	James Bridie	Laurence Neal
Everyman In His Humour	Ben Johnson	Pauline Graham
(at the Guildhall)		
Revue:		
Variations on a Theme	Barrie Grayson	Philip Berridge

1957/58

I am a Camera	John Van Druten	Victor Bonfield
Book of the Month	Basil Thomas	Douglas Goodlad
The Heiress	Ruth &	
	Augustus Goetz	Emmie Bent
Shadow of Doubt	Norman King	Arthur Morris
Tiger at the Gates	Jean Giraudoux	Geoffrey Burton
Morning's at Seven	Paul Osborn	Laurence Neal
The Relapse	John Vanburgh	Pauline Graham
The Queen and the Rebels	Ugo Betti	Victor Bonfield
Macbeth	Shakespeare	John Graham
Winter Journey	Clifford Odets	Tom Johnson
Blithe Spirit	Noël Coward	Douglas Goodlad
Separate Tables	Terence Rattigan	James Wheeler

1958/59

Arms and the Man	Shaw	Emmie Bent
Romanoff and Juliet	Peter Ustinov	Alan Gayton

Night Must Fall	Tennessee Williams	Tom Johnson
The Moon is Blue	F. Hugh Herbert	Douglas Goodlad
Toad of Toad Hall	A. A. Milne	Victor Bonfield
The Same Sky	Yvonne Mitchell	Leslie Walker
Dear Charles	Alan Melville	Emmie Bent/ James Wheeler
Death of a Salesman	Arthur Miller	Geoffrey Burton
Under the Sycamore Tree	Samuel Spewack	John Chambers
A Dead Secret	Rodney Ackland	John Graham
Look Back in Anger	John Osborne	Douglas Goodlad
Arsenic and Old Lace	Joseph Kesselring	Laurence Neal

1959/60

Plaintiff in a Pretty Hat	Hugh & Margaret Williams	Philip Berridge
The Chalk Garden	Enid Bagnold	Geoffrey Burton
The Devil's Disciple	Shaw	Leslie Walker
The Rape of the Belt	Benn W. Levy	Alan Gayton
1066 and All That	Reginald Arkell	Douglas Goodlad
The Voice of the Turtle	John Van Druten	Neville Williams
The Rainmaker	N. Richard Nash	Roy Wright
The Two Gentlemen of Verona	Shakespeare	Pauline Graham
The Old Ladies	Rodney Ackland	James Wheeler
Waltz of the Toreadors	Jean Anouilh	Douglas Goodlad
The Offshore Island	Marghanita Laski	Neville Williams
Nude with a Violin	Noël Coward	Jack Findlay

1960/61

Who is Sylvia?	Terence Rattigan	Victor Bonfield
The Hamlet of Stepney Green	Bernard Kops	Geoffrey Burton
The Constant Wife	W. Somerset Maugham	Roy Wright
The Flowering Cherry	Robert Bolt	Alan Gayton
Charley's Aunt	Brandon Thomas	Neville Williams
The Seagull	Chekhov	John Graham

The Kidders	Donald Ogden Stewart	Douglas Goodlad
Simon and Laura	Alan Melville	James Wheeler
The Prodigious Snob	Molière	Neville Williams
Waiting for Godot	Samuel Beckett	Pauline Graham
The Remarkable Mr. Pennypacker	Liam O'Brien	Robert Martin
The Grass is Greener	Tennessee Williams	Douglas Goodlad
Under Milk Wood	Dylan Thomas	Roy Wright

1961/62

Roar Like a Dove	Storm	Geoffrey Burton
The Crucible	Arthur Miller	Neville Williams
The Millionairess	Shaw	Roy Wright
Five Finger Exercise	Peter Shaffer	Douglas Goodlad
Treasure Island	Stevenson/Fagan	Neville Williams
Hay Fever	Noël Coward	Herbert Mason
The Bridge of Sighs	Thomas Muschamp	Philip Berridge
Julius Caesar	Shakespeare	Alan Gayton
A Clean Kill	Michael Gilbert	Roy Wright
Chicken Soup with Barley	Arnold Wesker	Neville Williams
Angels in Love	Hugh Mills	David Lyall
The Long and the Short and the Tall	Willis Hall	Victor Bonfield

1962/63

The Wrong Side of the Park	John Mortimer	John Graham
Figure of Fun	André Roussin	Neville Williams
The Hostage	Brendan Behan	Laurence Neal
The Complaisant Lover	Graham Greene	Tom Williams
Alf's Button	W. A. Darlington	David Lyall
Waiting in the Wings	Noël Coward	James Wheeler
The Caretaker	Harold Pinter	Neville Williams
Twelfth Night	Shakespeare	Pauline Graham
Billy Liar	Keith Waterhouse & Willis Hall	Neville Williams

Three	John Mortimer, N. F. Simpson, Harold Pinter	Derek Townend Geoffrey Sharp John Northam
Salad Days	Dorothy Reynolds/ Julian Slade	Douglas Goodlad
A Man for All Seasons	Robert Bolt	Alan Gayton
The Amorous Prawn	Anthony Kimmins	Derek Burrows

1963/64

Pools Paradise	Philip King	David Lyall
The Miracle Worker	William Gibson	Neville Williams
Summer of the Seventeenth Doll	Ray Lawler	Victor Bonfield
Subway in the Sky	Ian Main	Herbert Mason
Puss in Boots	Alan Brown	Alan Gayton
Time and the Conways	J. B. Priestley	Roy Wright
Henry IV – Part I	Shakespeare	Geoffrey Burton
For Better, For Worse	Arthur Watkin	Geoffrey Sharp
Semi-Detached	David Turner	Philip Berridge
The Keep	Gwyn Thomas	Tom Williams
Sergeant Musgrave's Dance	John Arden	John Graham
Make Me an Offer	Wolf Mankowitz	Roy Wright

1964/65

The More the Merrier	Ronald Millar	John Guillain
Dark of the Moon	Howard Richardson/ William Berney	Geoffrey Sharp
Maria Marten	Brian J. Burton	Laurence Neal
Roots	Arnold Wesker	Pauline Graham
Aladdin	Thea Craine	Alan Gayton
The Tiger and the Horse	Robert Bolt	Roy Wright
Hamlet	Shakespeare	Geoffrey Burton
Fallen Angels	Noël Coward	Neville Williams
The Cocktail Party	T. S. Eliot	John Graham
Tons of Money	Will Evans & Valentine	Geoffrey Sharp
Luther	John Osborne	Victor Bonfield

The Marriage-go-Round	Leslie Stevens	Clive Perry

1965/66

Amphytrion	John Dryden	Geoffrey Sharp
A Streetcar Named Desire	Tennessee Williams	Geoffrey Burton
Mr. Bolfry	James Bridie	Peter MacDowell
War and Peace	Leo Tolstoy/	
	R. D. MacDonald	Clive Perry
Mother Goose	Diana Bishop	Geoffrey Sharp
Lady Audley's Secret	Brian J. Burton	Laurence Neal
A Cuckoo in the Nest	Ben Travers	Herbert Mason
Saint Joan	Shaw	Victor Bonfield
The Farmer's Wife	Eden Philpotts	Pauline Graham
The Boy Friend	Sandy Wilson	Neville Williams
Mother Courage	Bertolt Brecht	Keith Miller

1966/67

My Three Angels	Sam & Bella Spewack	John Ghent
Chips with Everything	Arnold Wesker	Orry Pochin
Time Remembered	Jean Anouilh	Geoffrey Burton
Six Characters in Search		
of an Author	Luigi Pirandello	Geoffrey Sharp
Dick Whittington	Thea Craine/	
	Neil Bevan	Alan Gayton
A Doll's House	Ibsen	Sheena Rankin
Sweeney Todd	Brian J. Burton	Laurence Neal
A Midsummer Night's		
Dream	Shakespeare	John Ghent
The Gazebo	Alec Coppel	John Guillain
A View from the Bridge	Arthur Miller	Victor Bonfield

1967/68

A Severed Head	Iris Murdoch/	
	J. B. Priestley	Geoffrey Sharp
The Cherry Orchard	Chekhov	Geoffrey Burton
Summer and Smoke	Tennessee Williams	John Ghent
The Fire Raisers	Max Frisch	John Graham
Cinderella	Thea Craine	Alan Gayton

The Private Ear and The Public Eye	Peter Shaffer	John Northam
As You Like It	Shakespeare	John Ghent
The Cavern	Jean Anouilh	John Guillain
Oh What a Lovely War	Theatre Workshop	Laurence Neal
Dear Octopus	Dodie Smith	Victor Bonfield
Music Hall		Geoffrey Sharp

1968/69

The Killing of Sister George	Frank Marcus	Pauline Graham
The Workhouse Donkey	John Arden	Roland Joffe
A Month in the Country	Ivan Turgenev	John Ghent
On Approval	Frederick Lonsdale	John Guillain
Jack and the Beanstalk	Neil Bevan	Geoffrey Sharp
Who's Afraid of Virginia Woolf?	Edward Albee	Marcia Randle
The Homecoming	Harold Pinter	Keith Miller
Romeo and Juliet	Shakespeare	Brian Daubeny
No, No, Nanette	F. Mandel/ O. Harbach/ I. Caesar	John Ghent
The Right Honourable Gentleman	M. Bradley-Dyne	Douglas Goodlad
The Recruiting Officer	George Farquhar	Geoffrey Sharp
Music Hall		Victor Bonfield

1969/70

Diplomatic Baggage	John Chapman	Elvera Smith
The Taming of the Shrew	Shakespeare	John Guillain
Rattle of a Simple Man	Charles Dyer	John Hall
The Plough and the Stars	Sean O'Casey	Orry Pochin
Ali Baba	Neil Bevan	Geoffrey Sharp
A Scent of Flowers	James Saunders	Keith Miller
Hotel Paradiso	Georges Feydeau	John Ghent
Wait Until Dark	Frederick Knott	John Graham
Irma La Douce	J. More/D. Heneker/ M. Norman	Roy Smith

The Royal Hunt of the Sun	Peter Shaffer	Victor Bonfield
Say Who You Are	Keith Waterhouse &	
	Willis Hall	Douglas Goodlad
Old Time Music Hall		Geoffrey Sharp

1970/71

Hobson's Choice	Harold Brighouse	Victor Bonfield
Everything in the Garden	Giles Cooper	John Hall
Uncle Vanya	Chekhov	John Ghent
Zoo Story/Black Comedy	Edward Albee	
	Peter Shaffer	David Millhouse
Toad of Toad Hall	A. A. Milne	Douglas Goodlad
Dracula	Hamilton Deane/	
	John L. Balderston	Pauline Graham
Spring and Port Wine	Bill Naughton	John Guillain
Heartbreak House	Shaw	Keith Miller
Half in Earnest	Vivian Ellis	Roy Wright
Rebecca	Daphne Du Maurier	Victor Bonfield
The Prime of Miss Jean		
Brodie	Jay Presson Allen	John Ghent
Old Time Music Hall		Philip Berridge

1971/72

Boeing Boeing	Cannoletti/Cross	José Cooke
The Winslow Boy	Terence Rattigan	Martin Caven
Picnic	William Inge	John Ghent
Gaslight	Patrick Hamilton	Derek Burrows
Sinbad the Sailor	Thea Craine	Victor Bonfield
When We Are Married	J. B. Priestley	John Guillain
Belcher's Luck	David Mercer	David Millhouse
Inherit the Wind	Jerome Lawrence/	
	Robert E. Lee	Geoffrey Sharp
I Have Been Here Before	J. B. Priestley	Thea Craine
The Master Builder	Ibsen	Keith Miller
A Flea in Her Ear	Georges Feydeau	John Ghent
The Good Old Days		Roy Smith

1972/73

Relatively Speaking	Alan Ayckbourn	Ken Milton
All in Good Time	Bill Naughton	José Cooke
Hotel in Amsterdam	John Osborne	Keith Miller
Private Lives	Noël Coward	David Millhouse
Aladdin	Thea Craine	Philip Berridge
The Diary of Anne Franck	Frances Goodrich/	
	Albert Hackett	John Ghent
Not Now Darling	Ray Cooney &	
	John Chapman	Roy Smith
The Imaginary Invalid	Molière/Malleson	John Guillain
A Day in the Death of		
* Joe Egg*	Peter Nichols	Victor Bonfield
Ten Little Niggers	Agatha Christie	Tony Mortimer
The Rose Tattoo	Tennessee Williams	John Ghent
Old Time Music Hall		Geoffrey Sharp

1973/74

Quiet Week-end	Esther McCracken	Ken Milton
Forget-Me-Not Lane	Peter Nichols	Pauline Graham
Journey's End	R. C. Sherriff	Norman Brownjohn
The Little Foxes	Lillian Hellman	Neville Williams
Cinderella	Thea Craine	Roy Smith
The Chalk Garden	Enid Bagnold	Brian Daubney
The Secretary Bird	William Douglas	
	Home	José Cooke
Winter Journey	Clifford Odets	John Ghent
The Ghost Train	Arnold Ridley	Roy Smith
On-Act Play Festival, including		
Harlequinade	Terence Rattigan	Barbara Kenney
Vivat! Vivat Regina!	Robert Bolt	Derek Burrows
Old Time Music Hall		Thea Craine

1974/75

Dial M for Murder	Frederick Knott	John Saunders
Barefoot in the Park	Neil Simon	John Ghent
The River Line	Charles Morgan	Geoffrey Sharp
Bell, Book and Candle	John Van Druten	Peter Clay

The Melody Lingers On		Alan Mitchell
Humpty Dumpty	John Guillian & others	Roy Smith
The Bad Seed	Maxwell Anderson	Neville Williams
Arms and the Man	Shaw	Max Cotten
Cat Among the Pigeons	Georges Feydeau	John Ghent
Ladies in Retirement	Edward Percy/ Reginald Denham	Leslie Walker
The Skin of Our Teeth	Thornton Wilder	John Graham
Time and Time Again	Alan Ayckbourn	Barbara Kenney
Henry V	Shakespeare	Victor Bonfield
Palace of Varieties		José Cooke

1975/76

The Happy Apple	Jack Pulman	Peter Clay
Suddenly at Home	Francis Durbridge	John Saunders
Present Laughter	Noël Coward	Max Cotten
Detective Story	Sidney Kingsley	Geoffrey Sharp
The Wizard of Oz	L. Frank Baum	Alan Mitchell
Dangerous Corner	J. B. Priestley	Joanne Runswick
Major Barbara	Shaw	Pauline Graham
The Man Most Likely To	Joyce Rayburn	Peter Clay
The Member for Gaza	Benn Levy	Orry Pochin
Ring Round the Moon	Jean Anouilh	John Ghent
The Promise	Aleksei Arbuzov	Judith Pearson
Music Hall		Thea Craine

1976/77

Who's Pinched Me Tights?	John Guillain	John Guillain
Move Over, Mrs. Markham	Ray Cooney/ John Chapman	John Saunders
The Yellow Jacket	George C. Hazelton/ Benrimo	Barbara Kenney
The Lion in Winter	James Goldman	Orry Pochin
Signpost to Murder	Monte Doyle	John Ghent
Mother Goose	John Guillain	Roy Smith

Butterflies are Free	Leonard Gershe	Judith Pearson
Crown Matrimonial	Royce Ryton	Barbara Kenney
East Lynne	Brian J. Burton	Geoffrey Sharp
The Cat and the Canary	John Willard	Max Cotten
The Corn is Green	Emlyn Williams	John Saunders
Habeas Corpus	Alan Bennett	John Ghent
Old Time Music Hall		Joanne Runswick

1977/78

Who's Pinched Me Camel?	John Guillain	John Guillain
Let Sleeping Wives Lie	Harold Brooke/ Kay Bannerman	Alan Mitchell
Lady Windermere's Fan	Oscar Wilde	Geoffrey Sharp
The Dame of Sark	William Douglas Home	Judith Pearson
I Am a Camera	John Van Druten	John Ghent
Dick Whittington	Thea Craine/ Neil Bevan	José Johnson
The Day After the Fair	Frank Harvey	Neville Williams
The Man Who Came to Dinner	Moss Hart/ George Kauffman	Barbara Kenney
The Gentle Hook	Francis Durbridge	Joanne Runswick
The Magistrate	A. W. Pinero	John Ghent
The Hollow Crown	devised by John Barton	Orry Pochin
My Fat Friend	Charles Lawrence	John Saunders
The Circle	W. Somerset Maugham	Max Cotten
Music Hall		Thea Craine

1978/79

A Talent to Amuse	from Noël Coward	John Ghent
Don't Just Lie There, Say Something	Michael Pertwee	John Saunders
The Anniversary	Bill MacIlwraith	Peter Clay
A Public Enemy	Ibsen	Roy Wyse
Separate Tables	Terence Rattigan	Victor Bonfield

All for Your Delight		Kenneth Milton/ Thea Craine
Peter Pan	J. M. Barrie	Geoffrey Sharp
The Innocents	William Archibald	Neville Williams
Absurd Person Singular	Alan Ayckbourn	John Ghent
Arsenic and Old Lace	Joseph Kesselring	Elvera Smith
I Never Sang for My Father	Robert Anderson	Orry Pochin
Candida	Shaw	Pauline Graham
Hotel Paradiso	Georges Feydeau	John Ghent
Old Time Music Hall		Victor Bonfield

1979/80

A Funny Thing Happened on the Way To The Forum	Shevelove/Gelart	Roy Smith
In Praise of Love	Terence Rattigan	John Saunders
The Aspern Papers	Michael Redgrave	Max Cotten
Dear Brutus	J. M. Barrie	John Ghent
Jack and the Beanstalk	Thea Craine	Thea Craine
The Dark at the Top of the Stairs	William Inge	Neville Williams
Rookery Nook	Ben Travers	Elvera Smith
Entertaining Mr. Sloane	Joe Orton	George Spaul
Relative Values	Noël Coward	Roy Wyse
Murder with Love	Francis Durbridge	Alan Mitchell
The Glass Menagerie	Tennessee Williams	John Ghent
Jubilee Music Hall		Jacqueline Shuttlewood

1980/81

Who's Pinched Me Shirt?	John Guillain	John Guillain
Night Must Fall	Emlyn Williams	José Johnson
Chase Me Comrade	Ray Cooney	John Saunders
The Living Room	Graham Greene	John Ghent
Goody Two Shoes	Thea Craine	Thea Craine
The Heiress	Henry James/Goetz	Neville Williams
Noah	André Obey	Orry Pochin

Outside Edge	Richard Harris	Barry Starbuck
The Rivals	Sheridan	Leslie Walker
The Gingerbread Lady	Neil Simon	John Ghent
One-act Play Festival	organised by Alan Mitchell	
Grand Jubilee Music Hall		Thea Craine

1981/82

Oh What A Lovely War	Theatre Workshop	John Ghent
Absent Friends	Alan Ayckbourn	Geoffrey Sharp
Dark of the Moon	Richardson/Berney	Kathy Layfield
Can You Hear Me at the Back?	Brian Clark	Roy Wise
Cinderella	Thea Craine	Barry Starbuck
Clarence Day's "Life With Father"	Lindsay/Crouse	Neville Williams
What the Butler Saw	Joe Orton	John Ragg
Abigail's Party	Mike Leigh	John Ghent
Wings	Arthur Kopit	Neville Williams
The Rehearsal	Jean Anouilh	George Spaul
Shut Your Eyes & Think of England	Chapman/Marriott	Barry Starbuck
Music Hall		Alan Mitchell

Officers of the Leicester Drama Society 1922-1981

Date of AGM	President	Chairman	Honorary Secretary	Honorary Treasurer
1922	Dr. Rattray	(office of	Frank Clewlow	H. E. Winks
1923	Dr. Rattray	Chairman was	Frank Clewlow	H. E. Winks
1924	Dr. Rattray	not so called	R. G. Waddington	H. E. Winks
1925	H. Percy Gee	until 1927)	Geoffrey Mead	H. E. Winks
1926	H. Percy Gee		Geoffrey Mead	H. E. Winks
1927	W. Bastard	'Chairman of Executive' H. Pochin	Geoffrey Mead	H. W. Winks
1928	W. Bastard	H. Pochin	Geoffrey Mead	H. E. Winks
1929	W. Bastard	H. Pochin	Geoffrey Mead	H. E. Winks
1930	W. Bastard	H. Pochin	Geoffrey Mead	H. E. Winks
1931	W. Bastard	H. Pochin	Geoffrey Mead	H. E. Winks
1932	W. Bastard	H. Pochin	Moyra Haywood	H. E. Winks
1933	Sir Arthur Hazelrigg, Bart	H. Pochin	Moyra Haywood	H. E. Winks
1934	Sir Arthur Hazelrigg, Bart	H. Pochin	Moyra Haywood	H. E. Winks
1935	(left open)	H. Pochin	Moyra Haywood	Percy Kendall Percy Russell
1936	Mrs. F. L. Attenborough	H. Pochin	Moyra Haywood	
1937	Mrs. F. L. Attenborough	Geoffrey Mead	Moyra Haywood	Percy Russell A. E. Elkins
1938	Mrs. F. L. Attenborough	Geoffrey Mead	Moyra Haywood	Percy Russell A. E. Elkins
1939	No Meeting (Theatre Closed)			
1940	E. Gorham Gee	Geoffrey Mead	Moyra Haywood	Percy Russell A. E. Elkins
1941	E. Gorham Gee	Geoffrey Mead	Moyra Haywood	Percy Russell A. E. Elkins
1942	E. Gorham Gee	Geoffrey Mead	Moyra Haywood	Percy Russell A. E. Elkins
1943	A. Percy Groves	Geoffrey Mead	Marion Pickard (Deputy)	Percy Russell A. E. Elkins
1944	A. Percy Groves	Geoffrey Mead	Marion Pickard	Percy Russell A. E. Elkins

1945	S. Hibbert Russell	Geoffrey Mead	H. Roy Pochin	Percy Russell
				J. G. Hilton
1946	S. Hibbert Russell	A. Northfold	H. Roy Pochin	J. G. Hilton
1947	H. F. Henderson	A. Northfold	H. Roy Pochin	J. G. Hilton
1948	H. F. Henderson	A. Northfold	H. Roy Pochin	J. G. Hilton
1949	H. E. Pochin	A. Northfold	H. Roy Pochin	J. G. Hilton
1950	H. E. Pochin	A. Northfold	H. Roy Pochin	J. G. Hilton
1951	Frank Gayton	A. Northfold	H. Roy Pochin	J. G. Hilton
1952	Frank Gayton	A. Northfold	H. Roy Pochin	J. G. Hilton
1953	Geoffrey Mead	Frank Gayton	H. Roy Pochin	J. G. Hilton
1954	Geoffrey Mead	Frank Gayton	H. Roy Pochin	J. G. Hilton
1955	Frank Gayton	Geoffrey Burton	H. Roy Pochin	Fred Wincott
1956	Frank Gayton	Geoffrey Burton	H. Roy Pochin	Fred Wincott
1957	J. David Burrows	Geoffrey Burton	H. Roy Pochin	Fred Wincott
1958	J. G. Hilton	Geoffrey Burton	Alan W. Gayton	Fred Wincott
1959	J. G. Hilton	Geoffrey Burton	Alan W. Gayton	Fred Wincott
1960	H. Roy Pochin	Geoffrey Burton	Alan W. Gayton	Roger Ashwell
1961	H. Roy Pochin			
	A. Northfold	Geoffrey Burton	Alan W, Burton	Roger Ashwell
1962	A. Northfold	Geoffrey Burton	Alan W. Gayton	Roger Ashwell
1963	Frank Cooper			
	Watson	Geoffrey Burton	Alan W. Gayton	Roger Ashwell
1964	Frank Cooper			
	Watson	Geoffrey Burton	Alan W. Gayton	Roger Ashwell
1965	Dr. Elfed Thomas	Geoffrey Burton	Alan W. Gayton	Roger Ashwell
1966	Dr. Elfed Thomas	Geoffrey Burton	Alan W. Gayton	Roger Ashwell
1967	Ivan Tarratt	Geoffrey Burton	Alan W. Gayton	Roger Ashwell
1968	Ivan Tarratt	Geoffrey Burton	Alan W. Gayton	Roger Ashwell
1969	Gilbert Gillard	H. Orry Pochin	Victor Bonfield	Roger Ashwell
1970	Gilbert Gillard	H. Orry Pochin	Victor Bonfield	Trevor Brook
1971	Gilbert Gillard	H. Orry Pochin	Victor Bonfield	Trevor Brook
1972	Mary Angrave	H. Orry Pochin	Victor Bonfield	Trevor Brook
1973	Mary Angrave	R. Nigel Pochin	Victor Bonfield	Trevor Brook
1974	Alan W. Gayton	R. Nigel Pochin	Victor Bonfield	Trevor Brook
1975	Alan W. Gayton	R. Nigel Pochin	Victor Bonfield	Trevor Brook
1976	Pauline Graham	R. Nigel Pochin	Victor Bonfield	Trevor Brook
1977	Pauline Graham	R. Nigel Pochin	Alan Johnson	Trevor Brook
1978	Jack Roberts	R. Nigel Pochin	Alan Johnson	Trevor Brook
1979	Jack Roberts	Victor Bonfield	Alan Mitchell	Trevor Brook
1980	Leslie Walker	Victor Bonfield	Alan Mitchell	Trevor Brook
1981	Leslie Walker	Victor Bonfield	Alan Mitchell	Trevor Brook

Note:

If an Honorary Membership Secretary is elected he serves as an Officer of the Society. Frank Cooper Watson held this office for more than twenty years; but it is now vacant.